MANUAL FOR
PHYSICAL
THERAPY
TECHNICIANS

WILLIBALD NAGLER, M.D., F.A.C.P.

Physiatrist-in-Chief, The New York Hospital-Cornell Medical Center
Associate Professor of Medicine, Cornell University Medical College

YEAR BOOK MEDICAL PUBLISHERS, INC.
35 East Wacker Drive/Chicago

Library of Congress Catalog Card Number: 73-94398
International Standard Book Number: 0-8151-6312-6

FOREWORD

THE UNITED STATES is now engaged in a major attempt to reform the health system in ways that will make services more accessible, more uniform in quality, and more reasonable in cost. In considering the best means of improving the system, attention often turns to the matter of manpower and its distribution. Much thought has been given to how to train professionals to do their appointed tasks, how not to overtrain them, and how to redefine tasks so that the best possible use will be made of all categories of health workers.

It seems to me that the health industry as a whole can point with pride to the orderly and rational way in which tasks are assigned among the various types of professionals working within the area of rehabilitative medicine. If the rest of the health world could follow the example set by this specialty, one part of the problem with the medical system would at least be reduced.

This excellent book by Doctor Nagler will serve to instruct a large number of physical therapy technicians and other health professional students in the various modalities of treatment available for patients with debilitating and chronic illnesses. Many of these services, if rendered by doctors or physical therapists, would be far more expensive. They would also demand time from those professionals that could be better spent on the more complicated aspects of medical care. In his book, Dr. Nagler brings together in a new collection, written in clear and simple language, a host of well-established technics that can be made available to more sufferers from chronic diseases by physical therapy technicians.

When one combines this dimension of Dr. Nagler's effort with the fact that chronic, long-term care constitutes a major portion of the total medical enterprise, the importance of this book becomes apparent. It signifies the kind of approach that is needed to solve the pressing problems of health care in this country.

December 3, 1973
Washington, D.C.

JOHN R. HOGNESS, M.D.
President
Institute of Medicine
National Academy of Sciences

PREFACE

THIS MANUAL is written as a study guide for the physical therapy technician who is called upon to aid in the care of a patient with impaired function of the trunk or limbs. The book may also be useful as a guide for other health personnel, such as visiting nurses, rehabilitation aides and medical students who take summer employment in long-term care facilities.

The inability of persons to move around freely and perform the activities of daily living without the help of their fellowmen is not only an emotional but also an economic burden. Personal services are expensive.

It is no easy task to teach a person with impaired function of arms or legs a certain physical skill. It takes much patience and perseverance on the part of the teacher. There is, however, hardly any more grateful patient than the one who regains his ability to walk and move around independently.

The book outlines the various technics and principles that are applied to help persons with impaired function to gain independence in walking and in moving from one place to the other in spite of their disabilities. Some patients who suffer from a disease of the blood vessels may have to undergo surgery in which the affected part of the lower extremity is removed. These patients need training with artificial limbs. The manual outlines the more commonly used forms of amputations and gait training with the corresponding artificial limbs.

Elderly people often suffer a fracture of the hip when they fall. Orthopedic surgeons are now able to implant artificial hips and knees in patients who had become unable to walk because of severe degenerative changes in these joints. This manual outlines the principles of the various surgical fixation procedures after a fracture and the principles of joint replacement. After the surgical procedures have been performed, often a lengthy and intensive rehabilitation effort is necessary. The manual shows the more pertinent features of such rehabilitation programs.

The contents of the book are not original or new. They are the fruit of the experience of therapists who use such technics daily when they render care to their patients.

W. NAGLER.

TABLE OF CONTENTS

INTRODUCTION

The physical therapy technician is an essential member of the rehabilitation team. Medical rehabilitation is a specialty that concerns itself with improving the functional capacity of patients who, for one reason or another, have been left with impaired motion of an arm or leg or with impaired balance or coordination.

The major part of the rehabilitation service is rendered to the patient after the acute phase of the illness has subsided. Some rehabilitation services, however, are rendered during the acute phase of an illness—for instance, special breathing exercises or exercises to maintain range of motion in the joints. After the acute phase of the disease is overcome and the danger to life has passed, many patients face partial or complete loss of function of an extremity or damage to a part of the nervous system that affects normal body movement and the ability of the patient to function in his environment. It is mainly damage to a part of the nervous, vascular or skeletal system that causes disabilities. Often patients cannot return to their homes or places of work unless they regain some of the functions which have been lost. For instance, they may not be able to walk up the stairs, or they may need assistance in dressing. During a day's time we perform innumerable functions with our arms and legs without necessarily concentrating on them. After some function of part or all of an extremity, or even of a joint, is lost, we become aware how important each part of our body is. For instance, the loss of some ankle motion because of nerve damage makes walking very difficult. The loss of function of one hand eliminates any activity that is performed with both hands, like cutting meat. In order to regain some of the function, it is necessary that persons receive exercise training to strengthen an arm or leg, or they may need training in the use of a cane or crutch to enable them to walk again. Some joints may have to be supported or stabilized by braces.

The loss of bodily function brings with it feelings of inadequacy and despair, and often dependence on the help of one's fellowmen. To minimize the disability and to plan a way of daily living that is optimal for the patient is the task of a rehabilitation team. Such a team consists of a physician trained in rehabilitation medicine, a physical therapist, an occupational therapist and a social worker.

The physical therapist is a graduate of a physical therapy school. He has acquired special knowledge in kinesiology, in therapeutic exercises, in training with artificial limbs and walking aids and in the application

1

of other physical therapeutic agents such as heat, cold and electric currents.

The occupational therapist, a graduate of a school for occupational therapy, has expertise in making special equipment to facilitate the performance of daily activities. He analyzes bodily maneuvers step by step and trains the patient in such a manner that he can compensate for weakness or paralysis of a limb. For instance, the occupational therapist teaches the patient how to get into and out of a bathtub, how to cut meat in case one arm is damaged or how to use a weakened arm to support the good arm for bimanual activities. He also designs special equipment to compensate for loss of range of motion of a joint. For instance, loss of shoulder motion may require a comb with a long handle for combing the hair, or an enlarged handle for a spoon or fork may be needed to facilitate grip by a weakened hand.

The social worker is also essential for the effective functioning of a rehabilitation team. A social worker is trained in analyzing the patient's needs and desires and contrasts these with the means which the community, that is, the family or the society as a whole, can offer. For instance, the social worker will assist the patient or the patient's family in obtaining the provision of rehabilitation services or financial support from state or federal agencies. The social worker also makes arrangements for visits by the visiting nurses' service and for help by a homemaker.

The physician-in-charge outlines the rehabilitation program for the patient.

The physical therapy technician assists the physical therapist in his various duties. He is assigned a very specific task by his supervising physical therapist. For instance, he may be asked to teach the patient how to walk with crutches or to apply a heating modality to the patient.

To teach a disabled person the performance of a physical task may be very challenging. It requires much compassion and patience. The patient may be elderly, and the physical impairment may seem unsurmountable to him. He may need much encouragement and may have to be convinced that everything is not lost, that there is a chance for him to return to his home and friends and that the effort is worthwhile. A physical therapy technician must not be disappointed when a patient does not show any gratitude for all the efforts he has extended to improve the patient's condition. A physical disability may arouse bitterness in the patient toward his environment. He may feel that not enough is done for him. The physical therapy technician may often hear a patient's complaint: "I worked all my life, and now this must happen to me. Why do I have to be a cripple?"

Some of the patients you, the technician, will treat may also have some impairment of speech, the instrument of expression and desire.

This can cause frustration and feelings of inadequacy. The patient may have to write down his wishes on paper or use some form of sign language. Your patience may be challenged. It is in this critical situation that you have to show your human quality. Show the patient that you are concerned and be compassionate, but do not get personally involved.

The patient looks to you for guidance. Be very careful of what you say in front of him. Also, your uniform should be clean, and you should be well groomed and appear dignified. It is not only your technical skill but also your personality and appearance that have a beneficial effect on the patient's course. Remember, you may not achieve any improvement in your patient right away, and he may become easily discouraged.

In the event you cannot answer any questions asked by the patient, feel free to say so and explain that you have to confer first with your physical therapist. Never feel compelled to render a therapeutic regimen that you are not familiar with or not accustomed to, or that you are not certain you should do at this particular time. Confer first with your therapist. In case you are asked by a patient to do something that is contrary to the rules of the institution by which you are employed, do not involve yourself, and inform the patient that you are not permitted to do what he asked. It would not increase the patient's esteem of you if you acted contrary to the rules. In case you feel an exception has to be made, discuss the matter with your immediate superior.

As previously mentioned, a physical disability does change a patient's attitude toward his surroundings and toward his fellowmen. For instance, frequently parkinsonian patients become very timid. They do need much encouragement. Each activity they engage in takes a longer time and more effort than does the same activity in a normal person. Therefore, do not hurry the patient along. You will find much reward for your patience and effort as you see parkinsonian patients liven up under your program. You can see how, after treatment sessions, they walk, move and turn more easily. The speech of a parkinsonian patient is sometimes very faint and slow. You really have to give of yourself to listen to it. Also remember that parkinsonian patients tire very easily. They have to overcome rigidity when they initiate any motion. When the patient complains of fatigue, let him rest, and resume your program after 5–10 minutes.

Some patients may also have problems with their eyesight. Persons who have suffered a stroke may have their visual fields reduced. To have eye control over their motions, they have to turn their heads to the side of the impaired visual field.

Always keep in mind that the aim is not to make patients with impaired movement in a limb ambulate normally, or to restore completely normal anatomic function, that is, normal range of motion in a joint or normal strength. The most important part of your job is to make the patient able to function in his home environment without assistance or with minimal assistance from another person. The goal is to achieve the optimal improvement possible for the specific disability.

The attitudes you will encounter in disabled persons may range from overconfidence, as sometimes seen in multiple sclerosis, to timidity, bitterness and despair. The overconfident ones have to be shown their limitations; the timid ones have to be guided and encouraged. Those who are riddled with bitterness should be made aware that they are not the only ones stricken with the disease and that the personnel makes sincere efforts to lighten their burden. The patient who is in despair may be the most difficult problem. He may show no desire to improve himself, and he may make no effort to participate in the program outlined for him.

Sometimes you may hear a fellow worker saying: "The patient is not motivated." Do not use this expression as a value judgment about the patient. The therapeutic personnel's function is not to make a judgment about the patient, but to help as much as possible.

The disabled person does have a modification of his body image. This consequently changes the nature of his relationship with other people. This change does cause an emotional stress and does exaggerate emotional reactions. In a patient who has suffered a sudden severe disability, a regression of behavior may be seen—he may temporarily regress to some immature childhood pattern. A disabled patient who already has overcome this regression may have a recurrence when the disability is a long-lasting or permanent one.

A patient under an active rehabilitation program should only be assisted by another person in the performance of daily activities as much as absolutely necessary. An overprotective approach to a disabled person may eventually increase his physical disability. The patient's physical potentials should be challenged continuously. He needs continuous encouragement to perform daily activities by himself. Of course, be always ready to help in case the patient needs you.

It is important that you make the patient feel secure. For instance, the wheels of a wheelchair have to be locked before the patient stands by himself or is helped to the standing position. Always protect a paralyzed limb. Do not let it dangle loosely when you move the patient. In case the patient has a urinary catheter inserted, take extreme care not to get the catheter caught on anything or pulled.

Always try to preserve the patient's dignity and self-esteem. For instance, do not leave a helpless patient uncovered in bed with all the body parts exposed.

It is a difficult but a very rewarding task to improve physical disability, and I do not know of any nobler task than helping to ease the burdens of the disabled.

CHAPTER 1

ANATOMY OF THE HUMAN BODY

The human body is made up of various structures. Each of these performs a certain task that is important for the body's proper function. The physical therapy technician needs to understand mainly the bony structures, including joints and ligaments, the muscles, the nervous system and the circulatory and respiratory systems.

The Skeleton

The framework of the bones makes up the *skeleton*. The bones of the skeleton (New Latin, from Greek neuter of *skeletos*, dried up, withered) provide body support, protect underlying organs and serve as levers for body motions.

Wherever bones come together, they form a *joint*. The bones of a joint are held together by *ligaments* (Latin "bandage," from *ligare*, to bind), which are strong, nonelastic bands of dense tissue. They give stability and limit the joint to a very specific range of motions.

The structures that produce movement are the *muscles*. Muscles have the ability to contract or shorten and to relax. They are attached to bones and run across joints. Either muscle contraction or gravity causes motion in the joints. A muscle must have a nerve supply and a blood supply. The nerve stimulates the muscle to contract, and the blood brings nourishment and oxygen to the muscle and carries away waste products.

The anatomic position is the point of reference when motions of the various body parts are described. In the anatomic position the body is erect with the palms of the hands facing forward (Fig. 1-1). Other postures have to be taken up to enable the body to perform the various physical tasks (Fig. 1-2). When an extremity, or part of it, departs from the anatomic position in a direction away from the body's midline, we speak of *abduction* (Latin *abducere*, to lead away). If it moves toward the midline, this is *adduction* (Latin *adducere*, to draw toward). When an extremity turns around its longitudinal axis, we call the motion *rotation* (Latin *rotatio*, from *rotare*, to turn). When the joint angle becomes smaller by motion of the corresponding bones, this is called *flexion* (Latin *flexio*, the act of flexing or bending). When the joint angle becomes larger, this is called *extension* (Latin *extensio*, a stretching out

5

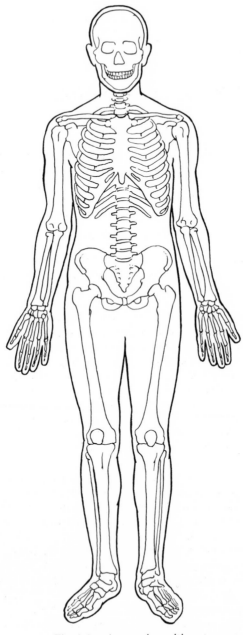

Fig. 1-1.—Anatomic position.

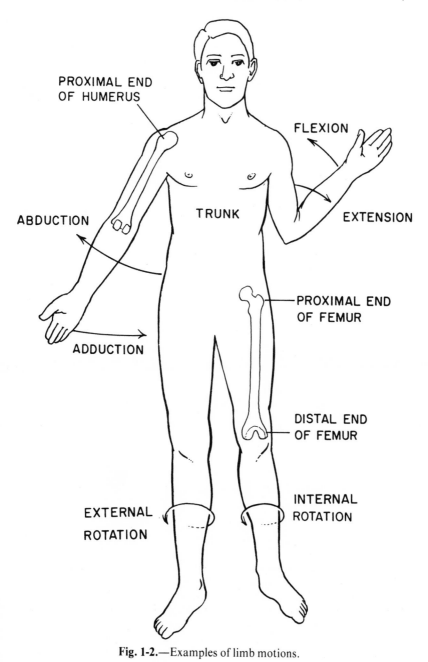

Fig. 1-2.—Examples of limb motions.

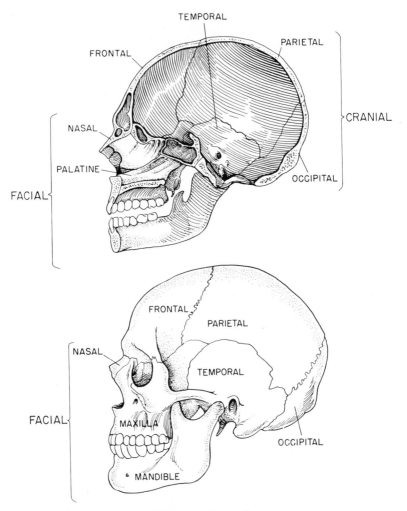

Fig. 1-3.—The skull.

or stretching further). The part of a body structure nearest the trunk is called the *proximal* end, the part farthest away the *distal* end. The front side of the body, that is, the side of the abdomen and the face, is called the *anterior* side, in contrast to the back, which is called the *posterior* side.

Groups of bones form specific skeletal units. These are the skull, the vertebral column, the shoulder girdle with the bones of the upper limbs, the thorax and the pelvic girdle with the bones of the lower limbs.

The Skull

The skull is divided into the cranial and facial parts. The cranial part contains the brain, which is a part of the central nervous system. The bones of the cranial part are the frontal, parietal, temporal and occipital bones. The facial part of the skull consists of the *maxillary bone* (cheekbone), the *mandibular bone* (chin), the *nasal bone* (nose) and the *palatine bone* (gum) (Fig. 1-3).

The Vertebral (Spinal) Column

The whole vertebral column has a total of 33 *vertebrae.* A vertebra is made up of a *body,* the solid round bone in the anterior part of the vertebra. Attached to each side of the body and joining in the back is the part called the *arch.* The main part of the arch of each side is the *lamina.* A projection on the lamina is called the *transverse process.* Posteriorly, there is a slender bony plate called the *spinous process* (Fig. 1-4). This is what we feel when we palpate the vertebral column with the patient bending forward. The space enclosed by the body and the arches of the vertebrae is called the *spinal canal.* It contains the spinal cord, which, together with the brain, forms the central nervous system. Between the bodies of the vertebrae lies a thick pad, called the *intervertebral disk,* which functions as a shock absorber.

The weight of the upper body is transmitted to the lower body through the vertebral column. The vertebral column consists of the following 5 sections: first, 7 cervical vertebrae, generally called the *neck.* The first 2 cervical vertebrae have a strikingly different shape from the remaining ones. The first one is called the *atlas* (Greek *Atlas,*

Fig. 1-4.—Vertebra.

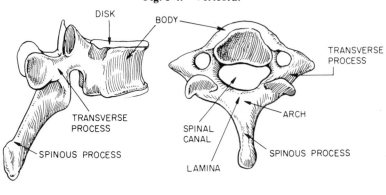

Side View   View from Above

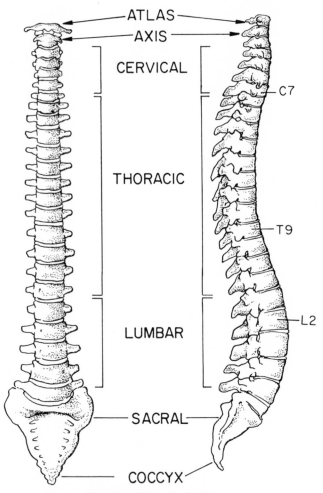

ATLAS

AXIS

CERVICAL

C7

THORACIC

T9

LUMBAR

L2

SACRAL

COCCYX

Fig. 1-5.—The spinal column.

the titan of Greek mythology who bears up the pillars of heaven), on which the skull rests. The second vertebra is called the *axis* (Latin, from Greek *axon*, axle). The head motions occur mostly around the axis. The remaining sections of the spine consist of 12 thoracic vertebrae (called the chest region); 5 lumbar vertebrae in the lumbar region (called the lower back); the *sacrum,* a bony plate made out of 5 vertebrae rigidly fixed to one another, and the 4 vertebrae of the *coccyx* or tailbone (Fig. 1-5). The sacrum and the hip bones together form the bony structure of the *pelvic girdle.*

The individual vertebra is designated by the first letter of the name of the section in which it is located. For instance, the ninth thoracic vertebra is designated T-9, and the second lumbar vertebra is L-2. There are 2 exceptions: the first two cervical vertebrae, as mentioned above, are called the atlas and the axis, respectively. The seventh cervical vertebra has the most prominent spinous process. It can be palpated easily through the skin.

The Thorax

The bones of the thoracic cage are the *sternum*, or breastbone, and the 12 pairs of *ribs*, which are attached posteriorly to the 12 thoracic vertebrae. Anteriorly, the upper 10 pairs of the ribs are connected to the sternum or breastbone by cartilage. The lower 2 pairs, called floating ribs, are free at their anterior ends (Fig. 1-6). The function of the thorax

Fig. 1-6.—The thoracic cage.

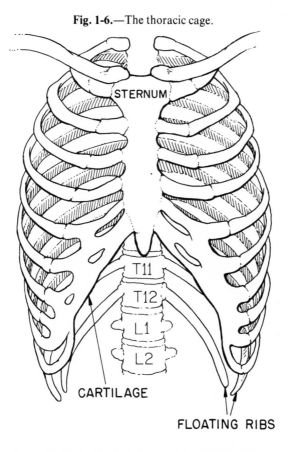

is to provide a rigid cage for the lungs. Furthermore, the rigid cage is able to increase and decrease the volume of the thoracic cavity, which is necessary for maintaining pressure difference within the thoracic cavity and the outside atmosphere.

The Shoulder Girdle and Upper Limbs

The main bony parts are the scapula, with a joint base for the upper arm, and the collarbone.

The *clavicle,* or collarbone, is an S-shaped bone in the anterior part of the chest. The proximal end is connected with the sternum and the distal part with the scapula. It serves for stabilization of the shoulder girdle.

The *scapula*, or shoulder blade, is a flat triangular bone located in the posterior part of the upper body. A ridge, called the *scapular spine,* extends posteriorly across the upper part of the scapula. The lateral end of this spine extends over the shoulder joint and is called the *acromion,* the highest point of the shoulder girdle (Greek *akron, extremity, akros,* extreme—denoting relation to an extremity, top or summit, or to an extreme— + Greek *omos*, shoulder). Below the acromion on the lateral

Fig. 1-7.—The shoulder girdle, posterior view.

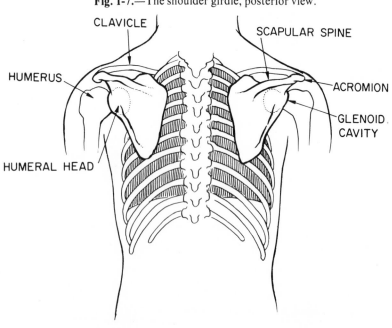

CLAVICLE

SCAPULAR SPINE

HUMERUS

ACROMION

GLENOID CAVITY

HUMERAL HEAD

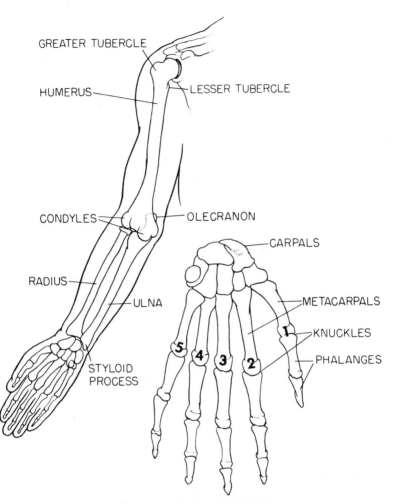

GREATER TUBERCLE

HUMERUS

LESSER TUBERCLE

CONDYLES

OLECRANON

CARPALS

RADIUS

ULNA

METACARPALS

KNUCKLES

PHALANGES

STYLOID
PROCESS

Fig. 1-8.—Upper extremity.

border of the scapula is a hollowed area, called the *glenoid cavity,* which provides the joint for the humerus. The scapula is held to the thoracic cage mostly by muscles. It serves as a base for insertion of trunk and upper arm muscles (Fig. 1-7).

The *humerus* is the bone of the upper arm. The upper, or proximal, end consists of the rounded head and a narrow part, the neck, and two prominences, the greater and lesser tubercles. The distal part flares out to form two rounded parts, called medial and lateral *condyles* (Latin *condylus,* Greek *kondylos,* knuckle).

The *radius* is a long bone of the forearm located on the lateral or thumb side. The proximal end of the radius is called the head.

The *ulna* is also a long bone of the forearm, located at the medial or little-finger side. The proximal end of the ulna is the sharp protusion of the elbow, called the *olecranon* (New Latin, from Greek *olekranon,* from *olene,* elbow + *kranion,* head, skull). The distal end forms a styloid process.

The *wrist* is made up of 8 small bones, the *carpal* bones (Latin *carpalis,* pertaining to the carpus, or wrist), which are arranged in two rows of four each.

The five *metacarpal* bones, which are cylinder-shaped, connect wrist and fingers. They are numbered 1 to 5, from the thumb to the little finger.

The *fingers* are formed by the *phalanges.* There are two phalanges in the thumb and 3 in each of the other fingers. A single bone of the finger is called a *phalanx* (Greek, "a line or array of soldiers"), and it is further designated by its proximal, middle or distal position. For example, the three bones of the little finger are the proximal phalanx, the middle phalanx and the distal phalanx (Fig. 1-8).

The Pelvic Girdle and Lower Limbs

The hip bone forms the sides of the *pelvic girdle* (Fig. 1-9). It has three parts: the *ilium*, which is the winglike part on the side with the bony ridge, called the *crest,* on top, the *ischium* and the *pubis.* These three parts join to form the hip socket, called the *acetabulum.* At the lower border of the ischium is the ischial tuberosity. When a person is sitting, these bony prominences carry the body weight. This bony prominence is very important for persons who have lost a leg due to injury or disease and wear a prosthesis or whose weakened leg has to be supported by a brace. The body weight is transferred onto the prosthesis or the brace through the ischial tuberosity (see Chapter 9).

The proximal end of the *femur* or thigh bone, together with the acetabulum, forms the hip joint. This proximal end, the *femoral head*, is connected to the femoral shaft through the femoral neck. Just distal to the neck there are two bony prominences, the greater and lesser trochanters. The greater trochanter can be felt by deep palpation on the lateral side of the hip. The femoral neck and the trochanters are often the site of hip fractures in older people when they fall. We speak about "femoral-neck" or intertrochanteric fractures (see Chapter 7).

The distal end of the femur forms the medial and lateral condyles which articulate with the *tibial plateau,* formed by the proximal end of the tibia. Both bones, together with the patella, constitute the *knee.*

The *tibia*, or shin bone, ends with a prominence proximally and

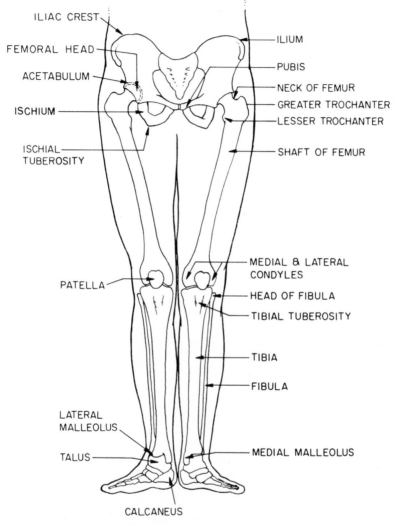

ILIAC CREST

FEMORAL HEAD

ACETABULUM

ISCHIUM

ISCHIAL
TUBEROSITY

PATELLA

LATERAL
MALLEOLUS

TALUS

CALCANEUS

ILIUM

PUBIS

NECK OF FEMUR

GREATER TROCHANTER

LESSER TROCHANTER

SHAFT OF FEMUR

MEDIAL & LATERAL
CONDYLES

HEAD OF FIBULA

TIBIAL TUBEROSITY

TIBIA

FIBULA

MEDIAL MALLEOLUS

Fig. 1-9.—Pelvic girdle and lower limbs.

distally. The proximal prominence forms, as just mentioned, the tibial plateau. On the proximal anterior surface of the tibia is a bony tubercle, the tibial tuberosity, for the attachment of the distal end of the quadriceps muscle tendon. The distal end of the tibia forms the medial malleolus, a part of the ankle joint. Together with the distal end of the fibula, it forms the mortise for the ankle joint.

The *fibula* is the long, slender bone on the lateral aspect of the leg. It is in contact with the tibia at its proximal and distal end. The proximal end is called the head and the distal end the lateral malleolus.

The *tarsus*, or ankle, is made up of 7 tarsal bones. The *calcaneus*, or heel bone, is the largest tarsal bone. It provides a major point of contact with the ground for transmission of body weight. In a normal gait, the stance phase starts with the heel strike (see Chapter 5). The *talus,* or ankle bone, is the second largest tarsal bone and is the most proximal of the group. It articulates with the distal ends of the tibia and fibula.

The *metatarsals* are a group of five bones that connect the tarsal bones to the toes. The metatarsals are similar in shape to the metacarpal bones of the hand and provide bony support for the toes. They are numbered 1 to 5, from the great toe to the little toe.

The toe phalanges are much shorter than the finger phalanges. There are two phalanges in the great toe and three in each of the other 4 toes. Toe phalanges are named in the same manner as are finger phalanges.

The Joints

Joints or articulations are formed wherever two or more bones come together. Most joints are bound together by *ligaments*, which are tough, nonelastic fibrous bands attached to the bones which form the joints. Muscles are secured to the bones by their tendons. Where muscles and their tendons cross a joint, they aid in joint stability.

Joints of the body are capable of various motions according to the structures involved. You will remember that when a joint angle becomes smaller than it is in anatomic position, this is called flexion. For example, when the elbow is bent, it is flexed. The opposite of flexion is extension. Thus, when the elbow is straight, it is extended. When a part is farther away from the midline than in the anatomic position, it is in abduction. For example, when the arm is raised out to the side, it is abducted. The opposite of abduction is adduction. A combination of these four motions, i.e., flexion, extension, abduction and adduction, is called *circumduction.* When a bone turns around its longitudinal axis, the motion is called *rotation.* The motion of turning inward toward the midline of the body is called *internal rotation.* The motion of turning out is called *external rotation.* These are the basic motions of the body parts. There are some other terms used to describe motion of body parts, for instance, gait deviations in amputees. Such terms are "hip-hiking," "vaulting," etc. (See Chapter 9.)

Throughout the body, there are various forms of joints. One of these forms is the *hinge joint.* The bone is at right angles to the horizontal axis of the joint, permitting motion in only one plane, flexion and extension, for example. The elbow and the finger joints are hinge joints.

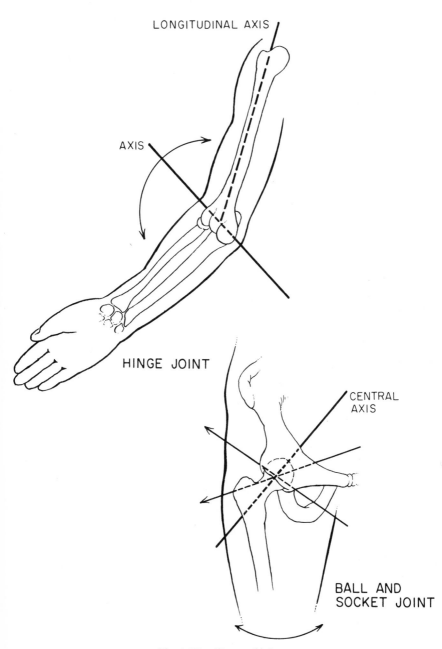

Fig. 1-10.—Types of joints.

In contrast to the hinge joint, which moves in one plane only, is the *ball-and-socket joint,* such as the hip and shoulder joints. In these, the ball-shaped head of 1 bone fits into the cuplike depression of another, permitting rotation around the central axis as well as movement in all ranges.

Besides the hinge joint, which only moves in one plane, and the ball-and-socket joint, which moves in all planes, there are other forms of joints with various degrees of motion within the bony framework (Fig. 1-10).

Specific Joint Motion

THE SKULL.—The only movable skull joint is the one formed by the temporal bone and the mandible, which is called the *temporomandibular joint* and is capable of flexion, extension, lateral motion, protraction and retraction (Fig. 1-11). All movements between skull, neck and trunk are made possible by the intervertebral joints of the vertebral bodies. The intervertebral joints are named and numbered for the 2 adjoining vertebrae that form the joint. For example, the joint between the fourth and fifth vertebrae is called the C4-C5 intervertebral joint in the cervical region, T4-T5 in the thoracic region and L4-L5 in the lumbar region.

HEAD AND NECK.—The occipital bone of the skull and the cervical vertebrae form the combination of joints that allows head and neck mo-

Fig. 1-11.—The temporomandibular joint.

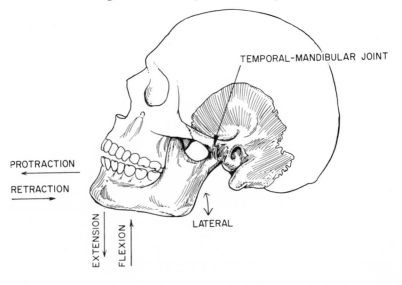

TEMPORAL-MANDIBULAR JOINT

PROTRACTION

RETRACTION

EXTENSION

FLEXION

LATERAL

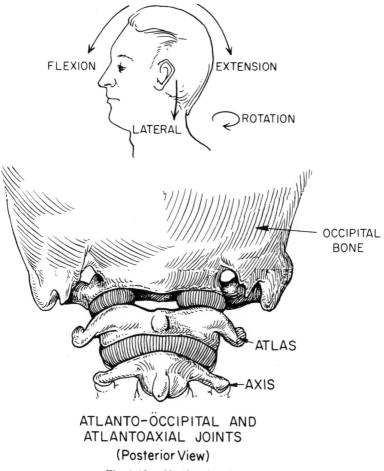

ATLANTO-ÖCCIPITAL AND
ATLANTOAXIAL JOINTS
(Posterior View)

Fig. 1-12.—Head and neck motion.

tion. These motions are flexion, extension, right and left lateral flexion and right and left rotation (Fig. 1-12). Most of these motions occur between the atlanto-occipital and atlantoaxial joints.

THE TRUNK.—The bones of the vertebral column form the joints of the trunk. The trunk is capable of the same motions as the head and neck, that is, flexion and extension, lateral flexion and rotation. Most of the trunk motion is performed in the cervical and lumbar area. There is no significant difference in the intervertebral joints of the various regions, but motion in the thoracic spine is limited by the rib cage.

SHOULDER GIRDLE

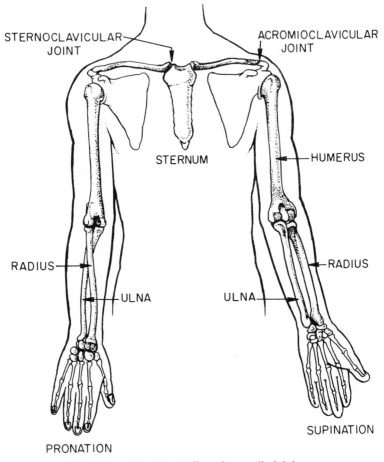

STERNOCLAVICULAR JOINT

ACROMIOCLAVICULAR JOINT

STERNUM

HUMERUS

RADIUS

RADIUS

ULNA

ULNA

SUPINATION

PRONATION

Fig. 1-13.—Shoulder girdle and upper limb joints.

THE SHOULDER GIRDLE AND UPPER LIMBS.—The shoulder girdle furnishes a strong movable base upon which the arms are attached to the trunk. The construction of the shoulder girdle is especially adapted for the performance of complex movements like overhead work. The shoulder girdle is composed of two joints, each named for the bones involved. They are the *sternoclavicular joint*, between the sternum and the clavicle, and the *acromioclavicular joint*, between the acromial process of the scapula and the clavicle. The shoulder girdle is capable of abduction, adduction, elevation, depression and rotation (Fig. 1-13).

The *shoulder* joint is a ball-and-socket joint, as already mentioned. The glenoid cavity of the scapula is the socket, and the head of the humerus is the ball. This joint is capable of flexion, extension, abduction, adduction and internal and external rotation.

The *elbow* is a hinge joint, as mentioned before. It is formed by the distal end of the humerus and the proximal end of the ulna, the olecranon process. The elbow is capable of 2 motions only, flexion and extension.

The *radioulnar* joints are pivot joints between the radius and the ulna. These joints allow a form of rotation of the forearm called *supination and pronation.* In the anatomical position the radius and ulna are parallel and the palm faces forward. This is a *supinated* position (Latin *supinatio,* from *supinare,* to lie backward or on the back). When the palm turns backward, the radius pivots over the ulna and the forearm is *pronated* (Latin *pronatio,* from *pronare,* to lie face downward).

The *wrist* is composed of the distal ends of the radius and ulna and eight carpal bones (Fig. 1-8). This joint is capable of flexion, extension, radial deviation and ulnar deviation (Fig. 1-14).

The *metacarpophalangeal* joints are between the metacarpals and the phalanges. They form the knuckles. These joints are numbered 1 to 5, from the thumb to the little finger. They are capable of flexion, extension, and a few degrees of ulnar and radial deviation. Spreading the fingers is called abduction; bringing the fingers together is called adduction.

The *interphalangeal* joints are between the phalanges of the fingers. Each finger, with the exception of the thumb, has three phalanges and a proximal (PIP) and a distal (DIP) interphalangeal joint. The thumb has only one interphalangeal (IP) joint. The IP joints are hinge joints and can therefore only flex and extend.

THE PELVIC GIRDLE AND LOWER LIMBS.—The *pelvic girdle* is designed for weight bearing and provides a rigid structure through which the weight is transferred from the trunk onto the hips. It has 2 joints, which are very limited in motion—the joint between the sacrum and the ilium, called the *sacroiliac joint,* and the joint between the right and left pubic bone, called the *symphysis pubis* (*symphysis,* Greek, "a growing together, natural junction") (Fig. 1-15).

The *hip,* like the shoulder, is a ball-and-socket joint, composed of the acetabulum, which is the socket, and the head of the femur, which is the ball. Analogous to the shoulder in its motions, the hip is capable of flexion, extension, abduction, adduction and rotation.

The *knee* is a modified hinge joint, composed of the condyles at the distal end of the femur and of the proximal end of the tibia (Fig. 1-16). It is enveloped in a capsule, its two cartilages called *menisci,* and is supported by strong ligaments and very strong tendons of the quadriceps

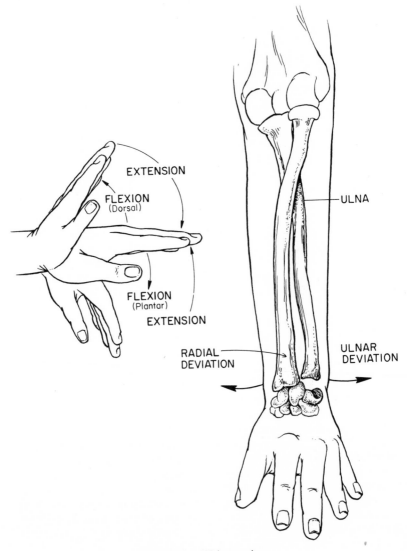

Fig. 1-14.—Wrist motions.

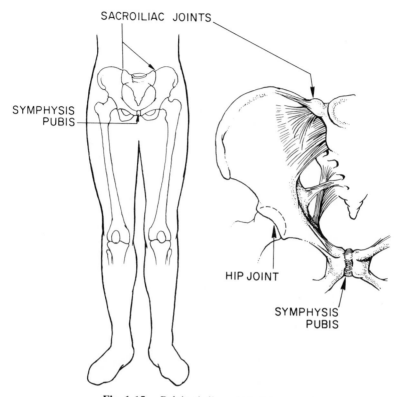

SACROILIAC JOINTS

SYMPHYSIS
PUBIS

HIP JOINT

SYMPHYSIS
PUBIS

Fig. 1-15.—Pelvic girdle and hip joints.

muscle. The principal motions of the knee joint are flexion and extension. In addition, a few degrees of rotation are possible.

The *ankle* is a combination joint. It is similar in composition to the wrist. The distal ends of the tibia and fibula form a mortise for the *talus*, which is one of the seven tarsal bones. The joints between the tarsal bones are sliding joints (Fig. 1-16). The combination of these joints allows flexion, extension, inversion and eversion.

The *metatarsophalangeal* joints between the metatarsals and the phalanges are similar to the metacarpophalangeal joints. The first metatarsophalangeal joint, which is the one for the great toe, is important in the toe push-off when walking (see Chapter 5).

The Muscles

Movements of the body are the result of gravity or the contraction of muscles. A knowledge of the major skeletal muscles of the body,

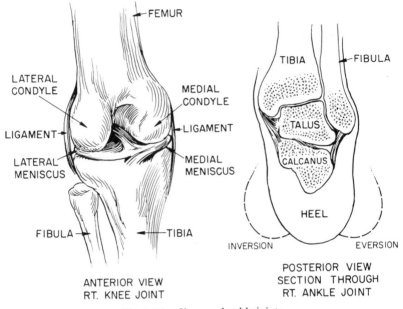

Fig. 1-16.—Knee and ankle joints.

including their location and relation to skeletal attachment and the motions they perform, is important for the physical therapy technician.

The location and action of only those muscles that the physical therapy technician will most likely be concerned with during his work will be listed.

The skeletal muscles are attached to the skeleton and are responsible for the movement of its parts. The muscles and bones together form a system of levers capable of producing various motions. A muscle is composed of many muscle fibers. These fibers are grouped and held together by connective tissues to form small muscle bundles. These connective tissues also contain blood, lymph and nerve supplies for the fibers. Groups of muscle bundles held together by sheaths called *fascia* (from Latin, a band, bandage) comprise the individual muscle. Each muscle is named according to its location, action or other distinguishing features. A muscle has a *belly,* or fleshy part, and a *tendon* on each side of the belly. The tendons are attached to the bones and are designated as the muscle's proximal or distal attachment (Fig. 1-17).

A muscle contracts when it receives a stimulus through the motor nerve. If the motor nerves supplying a particular muscle are destroyed by disease or injury, the impulse cannot be transmitted along the nerves, and the muscle cannot be voluntarily contracted. Muscle fibers

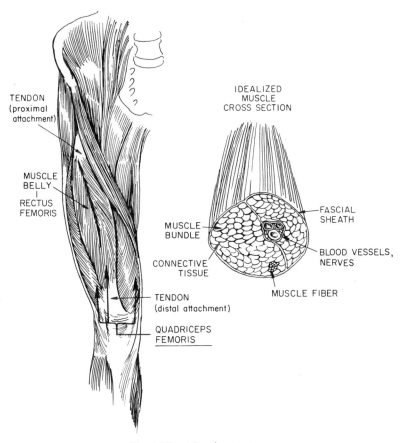

TENDON
(proximal
attachment)

MUSCLE
BELLY
|
RECTUS
FEMORIS

IDEALIZED
MUSCLE
CROSS SECTION

MUSCLE
BUNDLE

CONNECTIVE
TISSUE

FASCIAL
SHEATH

BLOOD VESSELS,
NERVES

MUSCLE FIBER

TENDON
(distal attachment)

QUADRICEPS
FEMORIS

Fig. 1-17.—Muscle structure.

diminish in size when they are not used. This wasting away or diminution in size is called *atrophy*. A muscle that is overdeveloped due to vigorous activity is called *hypertrophic*. Muscles seldom act independently. Even a very simple motion is usually the result of an interaction of a group of muscles. For each muscle group that produces one motion there is another group that produces the opposite motion, as, for example, flexion and extension.

MUSCLES OF THE HEAD AND NECK.—The strongest muscle in the skull is the *masseter* (Greek *maseter,* chewer) muscle, which is for chewing. One can feel the masseter muscle if one clenches the teeth together. The facial muscles enable us to wrinkle the forehead, to smile, to close the eyes, to frown and to perform other similar motions. The

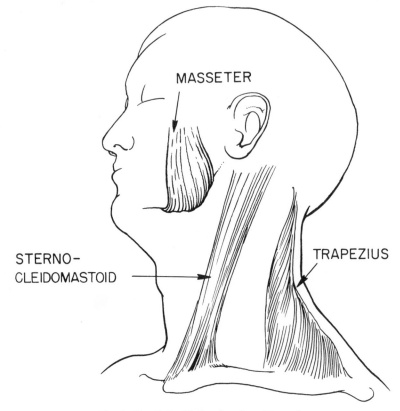

MASSETER

STERNO-
CLEIDOMASTOID

TRAPEZIUS

Fig. 1-18.—Palpable head and neck muscles.

more important muscles of the neck are the sternocleidomastoid muscle, which turns the neck, and the trapezius muscles, which permit shoulder shrugging. The belly of the sternocleidomastoid muscle can be felt on the left when the neck is turned to the right (Fig. 1-18), and it can be felt on the right when the neck is turned to the left. The belly of the trapezius muscle can be felt when the shoulders are shrugged upward.

TRUNK MUSCLES.—Some of the larger muscles of the trunk are the *erector spinae* muscles, which are attached to the vertebrae and help to keep the spine erect, and the *quadratus lumborum* muscles, which are attached to the iliac crest and the vertebrae. The latter are also called the "hip hikers," since contraction of these muscles effects hiking up of the hip (see Chapter 9) (Fig. 1-19). The main muscles of the trunk that lift the ribs during inspiration are the intercostal muscles, while the diaphragm muscles flatten the diaphragm in inspiration. When a person

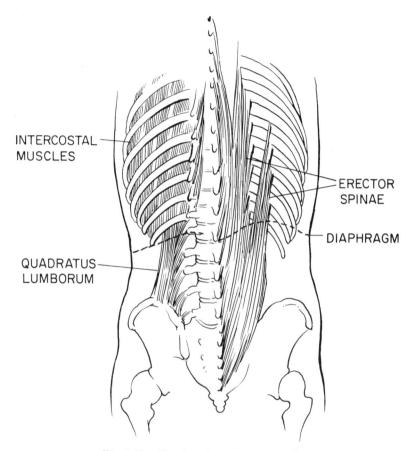

INTERCOSTAL
MUSCLES

ERECTOR
SPINAE

DIAPHRAGM

QUADRATUS
LUMBORUM

Fig. 1-19.—Trunk and respiratory muscles.

is very short of breath, other muscles, as the trapezius, sternocleidal or the latissimus dorsi muscles, participate in respiration (Fig. 1-20).

The abdominal muscles form part of the abdominal wall and aid forward flexion of the trunk when lying on the back (*rectus abdominis*) and in turning the trunk when the pelvis is fixed (*oblique abdominal* muscles) (Fig. 1-21). In a very muscular and thin person, the various segments of the rectus abdominis muscle can be seen through the skin.

MUSCLES OF THE UPPER LIMBS.—Muscles of the upper limbs include the *trapezius,* which helps to shrug up the shoulders; the *rhomboid* and *serratus anterior* muscles, which help to stabilize the shoulder and hold it to the rib cage, and the *deltoid* and *supraspinatus* muscles, which help to abduct the upper arm and hold the humeral head in the glenoid fossa.

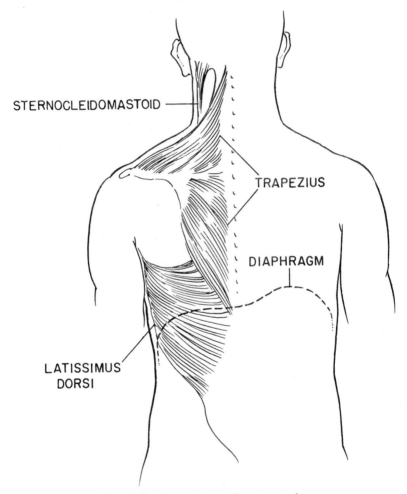

Fig. 1-20.—Accessory respiratory muscles.

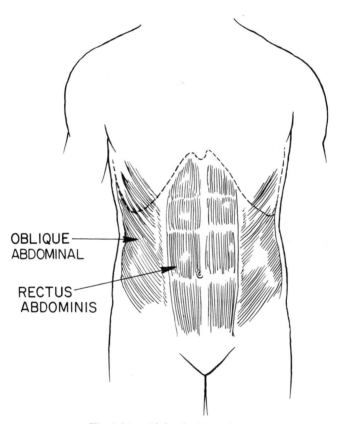

Fig. 1-21.—Abdominal muscles.

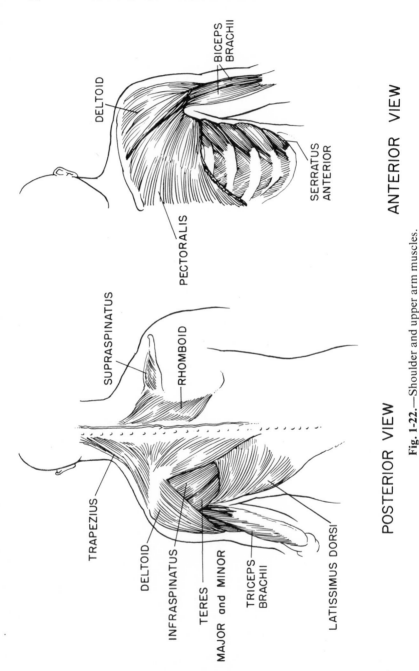

Fig. 1-22.—Shoulder and upper arm muscles.

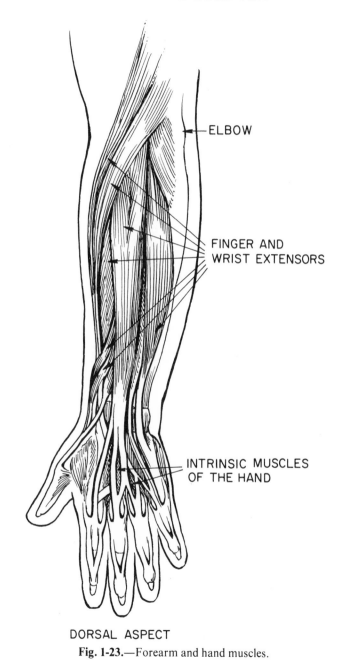

ELBOW

FINGER AND
WRIST EXTENSORS

INTRINSIC MUSCLES
OF THE HAND

DORSAL ASPECT
Fig. 1-23.—Forearm and hand muscles.

The *pectoralis* and *teres minor* and *major* muscles help to adduct the upper arm to the trunk. The *biceps brachii* helps to flex the elbow and move the upper arm forward, or anterior (Fig. 1-22). The *latissimus dorsi* is a shoulder depressor, and the *triceps brachii* is an elbow extensor. Therefore, the function of these latter two muscles is very important when ambulation aids such as crutches or walkers are used (see Chapter 8). In addition, there are the muscles of the forearm, wrist and hand. On the dorsal surface of the forearm are located the wrist and finger *extensors*. These muscles, in general, have their proximal attachment on the humerus and radius, and are attached distally to the carpal bones and phalanges. On the volar surface of the forearm are located the wrist and finger *flexors*. These muscles, in general, have their proximal attachment on the humerus and ulna and attach distally to the carpal bones and phalanges. In the hand proper, lying between the metacarpal bones and making up the fleshy part of the thumb and palm, is a group of muscles known as the *intrinsic* muscles of the hand (Latin *intrinsecus,* situated on the inside; situated entirely within or pertaining exclusively to one part) (Fig. 1-23).

Fig. 1-24.—Pelvic girdle and thigh muscles.

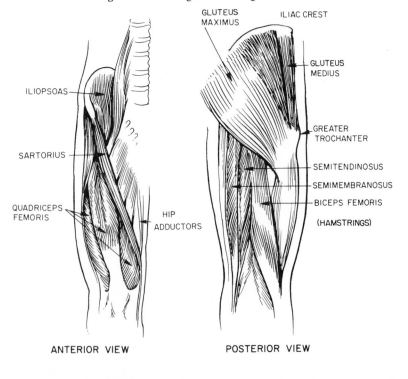

ANTERIOR VIEW   POSTERIOR VIEW

MUSCLES OF THE PELVIC GIRDLE AND THE LOWER LIMBS.—Muscles of these structures include the *iliopsoas, gluteii, hamstrings, quadriceps femoris, sartorius, hip adductor, gastrocnemius, soleus, tibialis anterior* and *peroneii muscles* (Figs. 1-24 and 1-25). In the foot, in addition to the tibialis anterior muscle, the long extensor muscles of the toes cross the ankle joint and cause dorsiflexion as well as toe extension. The iliopsoas muscle, which originates in the lumbar spine and inserts in the

Fig. 1-25.—Lower leg muscles.

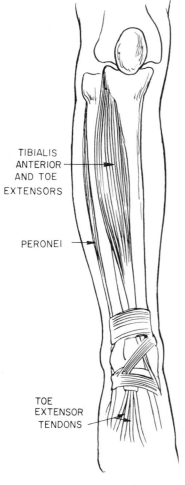
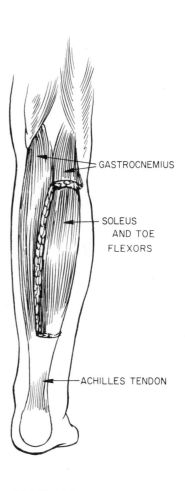

TIBIALIS
ANTERIOR
AND TOE
EXTENSORS

PERONEI

TOE
EXTENSOR
TENDONS

GASTROCNEMIUS

SOLEUS
AND TOE
FLEXORS

ACHILLES TENDON

ANTERIOR VIEW   POSTERIOR VIEW

thigh bone, helps to flex the hip. The gluteus maximus and medius, which originate in the iliac bone, a component of the pelvic girdle, and insert in the femur and its greater trochanter, extend and abduct the hip. The gluteus medius keeps the pelvis horizontal when in stance phase (see Chapter 8). The quadriceps muscle extends the knee. The gastrocnemius, which originates in the upper tibia and inserts with the Achilles tendon into the calcaneus, is very important in walking. By contraction, it effects plantar flexion of the foot and enables toe push-off at the end of the stance phase. The quadriceps femoris muscle is very important for knee extension and enables us to walk upstairs and downstairs (see Chapter 8). Posteriorly, the long flexor muscles of the toes also assist the gastrocnemius and soleus in plantar flexion. On the lateral side of the leg, the peroneii muscles run the tendons behind the lateral malleolus and cause eversion of the ankle. The tibialis anterior muscle effects dorsiflexion and inversion of the ankle.

Kinesiology

Kinesiology (Greek *kinesis,* movement) is the sum of what is known regarding human motion. Under the heading "Physiology of the Voluntary Muscles" (Chapter 2), only those areas of kinesiology that are important to the work of a physical therapy technician will be discussed. The movement of the body by its muscles is an intricate, complex activity depending on physiologic processes and intact joints, bones, nerves and muscles. Malfunction of any of these processes affects motion. There are several books available that give further insight into anatomic and kinesiologic problems.[1,2,3]

REFERENCES

1. Steindler, A.: *Kinesiology of the Human Body Under Normal and Pathological Conditions* (3d ed.; Springfield, Ill.: Charles C Thomas, Publisher, 1973).
2. Brunnstrom, S.: *Clinical Kinesiology* (3d ed.; Philadelphia: F. A. Davis Company, 1972).
3. Rosse, C., and Clawson, D. K.: *Introduction to the Musculoskeletal System* (New York: Harper & Row Publishers, Inc., 1970).

CHAPTER 2

PHYSIOLOGY

The word "physiology" (Greek *physis,* nature + *logos*, word, reason) is used to name the science that describes the physical and chemical events constantly taking place in the human body. Each of the major body systems has its very characteristic physiologic processes.

Physiology of the Voluntary Muscles

Muscular contraction is influenced by a variety of events. Some of the most important considerations are listed here.

NERVE SUPPLY.—Some form of stimulus is necessary to initiate muscle contraction. Muscular activity does not actually originate in the motor area of the brain but is associated with sensory inputs. Sensory impulses, such as taste, vision or touch, are integrated after reaching the brain, and the results of these integrations influence the type of muscular activity performed. Previous sensory experiences are stored in the brain and influence the pattern of response. In voluntary contraction of a muscle, the stimulus is provided by the impulse originated in the motor area of the brain. The impulse is conducted by the nervous system to the muscle. Any interruption or impairment of the normal pathway over which the impulse travels will result in abnormal patterns of motion or in failure of muscle response, which is paralysis. Similarly, injury or disease of the joint, muscle or bone will alter the smooth integrated motion normally seen, and an abnormal pattern of motion, such as incoordination, imbalance or weakness, is the result.

ENERGY SUPPLY AND END PRODUCT REMOVAL.—To enable the muscle tissue to contract after a stimulus is received from the motor nerve, an energy supply in the form of glucose and oxygen is needed. This supply is brought to the muscle tissue by the blood flow in the capillaries. At the same time the end products of the physiologic processes, such as carbon dioxide or lactic acid, have to be removed from the muscle tissue as waste products. The venous circulation and the lymph glands accomplish this task. The more active contractions of the muscle occur, the higher becomes the demand for energy supply. Any deficiency in the supply of glucose and oxygen impairs muscle

35

activity. Also, accumulation of waste products caused by an impairment in the venous or lymph system impairs muscular activity.

GRAVITY.—In all movements, the force of gravity plays a role. Gravity can either facilitate or impede muscular action. For example, in a standing position elbow flexion is against gravity, since the biceps must lift the weight of the forearm, but extension is accomplished by gravity. In a prone position, the effect of gravity reverses this situation.

EXERCISE AND FATIGUE.—During exercise, the carbon dioxide and lactic acid that are end products of metabolism increase in the muscle tissue, causing fatigue. Fatigue is partially the result of the body's inability to expel excess amounts of these accumulated end products. Continued exercise increases the gap between oxygen supply and demand, thereby hastening fatigue. Physical activity will result in fatigue more readily when the exercising muscles are weakened or otherwise impaired by disease or injury.

MUSCLE ACTION IN SPECIFIC DAILY ACTIVITIES.—The activities which follow are performed without effort by a healthy person. However, they may be a challenge to a person with paralysis, incoordination or limitation of motion. A person who is afflicted with some ailment that causes loss of skilled, well-integrated muscle action or loss of strength may need much muscular re-education and training to master a seemingly simple task.

Standing erect.—Erect posture is maintained by the balance and interplay of muscle groups. The extensors of the trunk and the hip are usually the most active muscles because they work against the pull of gravity. They are often termed the *antigravity* muscles. These muscles are the extensors of the neck, back, hip and knee and the plantar flexors of the ankle. Calf muscle interplay is very important. A paralysis, weakness or tightness of any muscle used in standing erect affects posture or the ability to maintain an erect, standing position. For example, standing is precarious for patients with paralysis of the muscles that extend hips and knees.

Walking.—In walking, one leg swings forward while the other leg supports the body. Weakness, paralysis, or tightness of any of the muscles used in walking may cause limping or an alteration in the walking pattern. For example, a patient with paralysis of the dorsal flexors of the foot has to lift the leg high to prevent stubbing the toes. Pain is also a cause of abnormal walking patterns. (See Chapter 5.) In general, the muscles used in walking are the following:

1. The extensors of the knees, to straighten the knees and prevent buckling when weight is taken on them, for instance in stair climbing.

2. The extensors of the hips and trunk, to keep the trunk from falling forward.

3. The abductors of the hips, to keep the unsupported side of the pelvis from dropping when the other leg is in swing phase (see Chapter 5).

4. The flexors of the hips, to bring the limb forward in swing phase.

5. The dorsiflexors of the ankle, to allow the foot and toes to clear the ground and prevent foot slap when the heel strikes the floor at the beginning of the stance phase.

6. The plantar flexors of the ankle, to permit toe push-off at the end of the stance phase.

In cases where there is a permanent or temporary impairment of the weight-bearing structures of the pelvic girdle or the lower limbs, weight bearing must be transferred to body parts which were originally not designed for carrying the body weight and have to be adapted to a weight-bearing function. With the aid of crutches, the shoulder girdle and upper limbs take over this function (see Chapter 8). Persons who have to use crutches for years develop very strong shoulder and upper arm muscles.

WALKING WITH CRUTCHES.—During crutch walking, the patient may have to carry most of his body weight with the shoulder girdle and upper limbs. The shoulder girdle, as mentioned before, is not adapted for weight bearing. The most important muscle groups used in manipulation of crutches are the following:

1. The flexors of the shoulders, to move the crutches forward.

2. The extensors of the elbows, to hold the elbow straight so that the elbow will not buckle when the body weight is placed on the hands.

3. The flexors of the fingers and thumbs, to permit grasping the crutches.

4. The flexors and extensors of the wrist, to provide stability and to keep the hands in the correct position on the handpieces.

5. The depressors and downward rotators of the shoulder girdle, to lift the body as the weight is transmitted by the arms pushing down on the handgrip of the crutches.

Physiology of the Circulatory System

The *circulatory system,* which consists of the blood vascular system and the lymphatic system, circulates blood through the entire body, supplying food and oxygen to the body tissues and at the same time removing waste products such as carbon dioxide. Knowledge of the blood vascular system helps the physical therapy technician to understand the problems of the patient who has defective circulation and to recognize important signs and symptoms of failing circulation while physical therapy procedures are being administered.

The vascular system, which transports the blood, consists of the blood vessels and the heart.

The *blood* is a body fluid that transports vital material and circulates constantly. The average person has approximately 5–6 L of blood in his body. Blood is approximately 50% plasma, the liquid part, and 50% solid substance, the cellular elements. Plasma is pale yellow and is made of water, mineral salts and proteins. The red blood corpuscles contain a pigment called *hemoglobin* (Greek *haima*, blood, + Latin *globulus*, diminutive of *globus*, a small, often minute spherical mass), a form of a protein. Hemoglobin consists of a globulin and an iron salt that make the blood red. It has the ability to combine with oxygen and carbon dioxide, carrying the former from the lungs to the cells and the latter from the cells to the lungs. Other solid cellular elements are the *white corpuscles,* or *leukocytes* (Greek *leukos*, white, + Greek *kytos*, cell), which are colorless. These can penetrate the walls of capillaries and enter the surrounding tissues. Their primary function is a protective one; they can ingest and destroy bacteria in the blood and tissues. Their number increases rapidly when an infection is present. Other cellular elements are the *blood platelets,* which are round or oval bodies. These blood platelets aid in *coagulation* (Latin *coagulatio*, the process of clot formation), or clotting of the blood.

Blood vessels form a network of tubes that allows the blood to circulate to all parts of the body. They consist of *arteries, capillaries* and *veins*. Arteries are elastic, muscular tubes that carry blood from the heart to the peripheral body parts. Near the heart, arteries are 2–3 cm in diameter. Farther away from the heart, the diameter decreases. Arteries have their own nerve supply, and their diameters vary during contraction and relaxation. Their terminal branches are called *arterioles* and are connected with the capillaries.

Capillaries are tiny, thin-walled vessels that link arterioles and veins. They form a dense interrelating network in the tissues of all parts of the body. Through their thin walls oxygen and food, which are necessary for the tissues, as well as carbon dioxide and other waste products that are to be carried away in the veins, can penetrate.

Veins are similar to arteries, except that they have thinner and much less elastic walls. They carry carbon-dioxide–loaded blood to the heart. Their terminal branches receive blood from the capillaries. As the veins approach the heart, they become larger in diameter. The vein that brings blood from the upper body parts to the heart is called the *vena cava superior,* and the one that brings blood from the lower body parts is called the *vena cava inferior.*

The *heart* (Fig. 2-1), a hollow organ with muscular walls, the *myocar-*

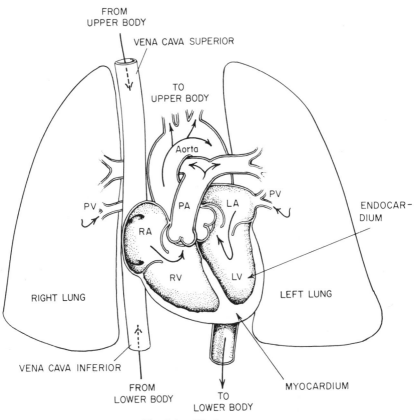

FROM
UPPER BODY

VENA CAVA SUPERIOR

TO
UPPER BODY

Aorta

PV

PA   LA   PV

RA

ENDOCAR-
DIUM

RV   LV

RIGHT LUNG   LEFT LUNG

VENA CAVA INFERIOR

FROM
LOWER BODY   TO
LOWER BODY   MYOCARDIUM

Fig. 2-1.—The heart.

dium, is in the anterior part of the chest behind the sternum. It functions as a pump. The heart's interior is divided into the right and left heart, each containing two chambers, the upper chamber or *atrium,* and the lower chamber or *ventricle.* The right atrium (RA) is connected to the large veins, the venae cavae, through which blood with carbon-dioxide–loaded red blood cells passes from the body to the heart. The left ventricle (LV) is connected to a large artery, the *aorta* (New Latin; Greek *aorte,* from *airein,* to lift, heave), through which blood is pumped from the heart to the body. The right ventricle (RV) is connected to the lungs by the pulmonary artery (PA). The pulmonary artery is the only artery in the human body which carries carbon-dioxide–rich blood. The left atrium (LA) is connected to the pulmonary veins (PV), the only veins with oxygen-rich blood, which carry blood from the lungs back to the heart after oxygen has been taken up by the blood in the lungs. The inner side of the heart has a membranous lining, the *endocardium,* which folds back to form the valves of the heart—the *tricuspid valve,* between the right atrium and ventricle, and the *mitral valve,* between the left atrium and ventricle.

The functions of the circulation and the blood are the following:

RESPIRATION.—Oxygen is carried by the hemoglobin in the red corpuscles. It is picked up by the red corpuscles, which contain hemoglobin, as these pass through the capillaries along the wall of the *alveoli* (Latin, diminutive of *alveus,* hollow) of the lungs. Carbon dioxide, the result of the utilization of the oxygen by the tissues, is carried back by the red blood cells to the alveoli of the lungs and breathed out of the body. The blood also carries food, like protein, fat and carbohydrates, after these have been absorbed by the blood from the walls of the intestines, to the tissues of the body. It also carries waste products to the kidneys for excretion in the urine. Some waste products are carried to other organs, such as the liver, to be made less toxic prior to excretion. The blood transports the water of the body tissues for maintenance of fluid balance. It regulates the body temperature. Blood distributes heat produced by the body, and, because of its water content and mobility, serves as a temperature regulator for the body (see Chapter 3). Heat locally applied will eventually be distributed into the body by the circulation.

THE BLOOD VESSELS.—The blood vessels carry blood to the tissues. Since the arteries receive blood from the heart, the arterial stream flows in spurts as the heart beats. The capillaries transmit food and oxygen to the tissues and receive waste products to be excreted from the body. The veins carry the blood from the capillaries back to the heart. The flow in the veins is smooth. Most venous flow is against gravity. The valves of the veins trap the blood so that it cannot flow backward. Active contraction of skeletal muscles helps to propel the blood from the lower body parts to the heart. The heart serves as a pump for the circulatory system. It contracts and forces the blood into the arteries, maintaining pressure in the arteries and controlling the rate of flow.

THE HEART-LUNG CYCLE (FIG. 2-1).—The deoxygenated blood flowing from the veins via the vena cava superior and vena cava inferior into the right atrium (RA) passes into the right ventricle (RV) and, by way of the pulmonary artery (PA), into the lungs, where the carbon dioxide is removed and oxygen is added. From the lungs, the blood passes through the pulmonary veins (PV) and enters the left atrium (LA). It then goes to the left ventricle (LV) and by way of the aorta into the arteries. This complex cycle occurs approximately 60–80 times a minute. The frequency can easily double when the oxygen demand of the tissues is increased by activity. When the heart muscle contracts, the blood is forced from the chamber into the arteries. This is called the *systole* (systolic pressure), from Greek *systole,* a drawing together, contraction. The phase of relaxation when the chamber fills with blood is called the *diastole* (diastolic pressure), from Greek *diastole,* a drawing asunder, expansion.

THE PULSE.—The pulse of the body is the contraction and relaxation of the arterial walls. A normal pulse is approximately 70–80 beats per minute. The pulse indicates the rate of the heartbeat as well as its rhythm.

BLOOD PRESSURE.—This is the pressure exerted by the blood against the wall of the artery. It is highest when the left ventricle contracts (systole) and lowest when the left ventricle relaxes (diastole).

The Respiratory System

The metabolic activity of the tissues of the body turns oxygen into carbon dioxide (CO_2). As a waste product, this must be eliminated. The process of oxygen and carbon dioxide exchange is called *respiration* (Latin *respiratio,* from *respirare,* to breathe). The respiratory system, together with the circulatory system, makes this exchange possible.

The *respiratory system* consists of the air passage and the lungs. The air passage allows the air to reach the lungs. It consists of the nose, pharynx, larynx, trachea and bronchi (Fig. 2-2).

THE NOSE.—The *nose* is the entrance of the air passage. It has 2 openings, the nostrils. The nasal cavity is partitioned by a septum and is lined with mucous membrane, which secretes a viscous fluid, called *mucus.* Air is warmed, moistened and filtered in the nasal cavity.

THE PHARYNX.—The *pharynx* (Greek) connects the nose to the larynx. In the walls of the pharynx are masses of lymph nodes called *adenoids* and *tonsils,* which are filters for bacteria from the outside. The pharynx is also the passage from the mouth to the esophagus (Greek *oisophagos,* from, *oiso,* to carry, + *phagein,* to eat).

THE LARYNX.—The *larynx* (Greek, "the upper part of the windpipe"), or voice box, consists of cartilages. The thyroid cartilage, or Adam's apple, is the largest cartilage and can be palpated and seen through the skin. It moves up and down when one speaks or swallows. When food is being swallowed, the *epiglottis,* a cartilage of the larynx,

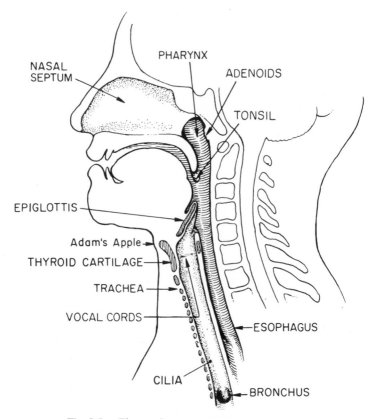

Fig. 2-2.—The respiratory system: upper airways.

closes its openings so that the food is forced into the esophagus and prevented from entering the lungs. In case food enters the lung, we speak of *aspiration.* If a piece of food enters the trachea, it causes choking. The larynx is crossed by two membranous bands, the *vocal cords.*

THE TRACHEA.—The *trachea* or windpipe (Latin, from Greek [*arteria*] *tracheia,* rough artery) is a tube whose lumen is held open by cartilaginous rings. It extends from the larynx down to about the level of the second rib, where it divides to form two bronchial tubes. The trachea is lined with mucous membranes and *cilia* (Latin plural of *cilium,* a minute vibratile, hairlike process attached to a free surface of a cell), which filter the air before it enters the lungs.

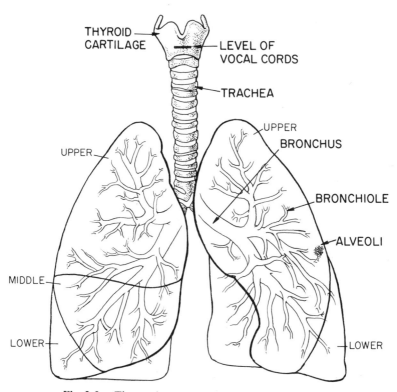

Fig. 2-3.—The respiratory system: trachea and bronchi.

THE BRONCHI.—The *bronchi* consist of two bronchial tubes. One bronchus enters each lung, where it branches into many bronchioles (Fig. 2-3).

THE LUNGS.—The *lungs* are the main organs of respiration. They are composed of a light, elastic, spongy tissue. Each lung is divided into sections or lobes. The right lung has three lobes, the upper, middle and lower lobes. The left lung has two lobes, the upper and the lower. On the left, the place of the middle lobe is largely taken up by the heart and the aorta. The bronchioli connect with the alveoli. Each lobe contains many *alveoli*, or air sacs, which are at the end of the bronchioles. These alveoli have elastic walls and thin linings that separate the capillaries of the wall from the air sac. It is in the alveoli that the exchange of oxygen from the outside air to the blood and of carbon dioxide from the blood to the air takes place.

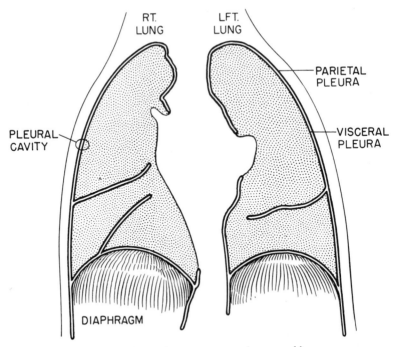

Fig. 2-4.—The respiratory system: pleurae and lungs.

Each lung is covered by a smooth membrane, called the *visceral pleura* which secretes the pleural fluid. In addition, the inner wall of the thorax and diaphragm are covered by the *parietal pleura*. The space between these two pleurae is called the *pleural cavity* (Fig. 2-4). The *diaphragm* separates the respiratory system from the stomach and the intestines.

The physiologic principle of respiration is as follows: *Inspiration* (Latin *inspirare*, from *in*, in, + *spirare*, to breathe) is an active movement during which the diaphragm lowers its dome to increase the capacity of the thoracic cage together with the elevation of the ribs. The pressure decrease in the increasing thoracic cavity and expansion of the lung tissue cause air to flow into the respiratory tract from the outside. *Expiration* (Latin *exspirare*, from *ex*, out, + *spirare*, to breathe) is a passive process as the relaxed diaphragm forms a dome upward. The rib cage is lowered by allowing the elastic recall of the structures and forces the air out of the lungs into the outside air. During forced expiration or during coughing, additional air is expelled at high velocity by contraction of the abdominal muscles. The increase of intra-abdominal pressure pushes the diaphragm further upward.

Normally an adult person breathes about 16 times a minute. When the respiration is fast, we speak of labored respiration. When the chest expansion is diminished, there is shallow respiration.

The Nervous System

The nerve functions are a highly complex system in the human body. The system makes it possible for the body to be aware of its surroundings, to coordinate its mental and physical activities and to respond as needed to stimuli. The nervous system may be divided into three distinct systems: central, peripheral and autonomic. Each part of this system carries out very specific functions.

The Central Nervous System

The *central nervous system* is composed of the brain and the spinal cord. These structures are covered by the *meninges* (Greek plural of *meninx,* membrane). The central nervous system receives all incoming optical, acoustic and tactile stimuli and coordinates the activities of the various body systems. It carries out all activities of learning, thinking and reasoning, and directs the voluntary action of the body.

The *brain* is the directional center for the entire nervous system. It is housed in the cranium of the skull. It is divided into two parts: the *cerebrum* (Latin, brain), which is the main part of the brain, and a smaller part, the *cerebellum* (Latin, little brain). The cerebrum is divided into lobes that are named for the corresponding bone of the skull protecting the individual lobe. The *frontal lobe* is the motor area and the center for movement, speech and writing; the *parietal lobe* is the sensory area for heat, cold, touch and pressure; the *temporal lobe* is the center for hearing and smelling, and the *occipital lobe* is the center for vision (Fig. 2-5). The cerebellum is located underneath the posterior part of the cerebrum. It governs the timing and integration of voluntary muscular movements, coordinates body activity, regulates muscle tone and is the center of reflex action and equilibrium.

The *brain stem* links the cerebrum to the spinal cord. It contains important tracts leading to and from the centers of the cerebrum and cerebellum. Many nerve tracts that carry stimuli from the various parts of the brain to the spinal cord cross from one side to the other in the brain stem. The crossing over of nerve tracts explains the fact that the impairment of arms and legs of a person with brain damage is on the side opposite to his injury. A respiratory center is also located in the brain stem.

The spinal cord, which is protected by the vertebrae, is made up of ascending and descending tracts that connect the brain to the peripheral

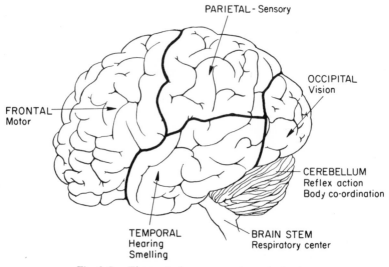

PARIETAL - Sensory

OCCIPITAL
Vision

FRONTAL
Motor

CEREBELLUM
Reflex action
Body co-ordination

TEMPORAL
Hearing
Smelling

BRAIN STEM
Respiratory center

Fig. 2-5.—The central nervous system: the brain.

nerves. It extends from the brain stem to the level of the second lumbar vertebra where the spinal cord ends. The peripheral nerve fibers to the hips and legs form the so-called *cauda equina,* or horsetail (Fig. 2-6).

Between the meninges and the structures of the central nervous system is the *cerebrospinal fluid.*

The Peripheral Nervous System

The *peripheral nervous system* is composed of nerves located outside the central nervous system. It is frequently designated as the lower motor neuron system, in contrast to the upper motor neuron system, which includes all structures of the central nervous system. The peripheral nerve system contains motor neurons that cause muscles to contract and sensory neurons that receive stimuli and relay them to the central nervous system. There are 12 pairs of cranial nerves, which supply the organs of special senses and part of the face, the tongue, neck, thorax and abdomen, and 31 pairs of spinal nerves, which innervate the skeletal muscles and give sensation in the trunk and upper and lower limbs. Nerves for the upper limbs coming from the spinal cord form the brachial plexus in the shoulder area.

The brachial plexus gives off five motor nerves from its three cords: the short *axillary* nerve to the deltoid muscle, which abducts the shoulder; the *radial* nerve, which effects extension of elbow, wrist and fingers; the *musculocutaneous* nerve, which flexes the elbow, and the

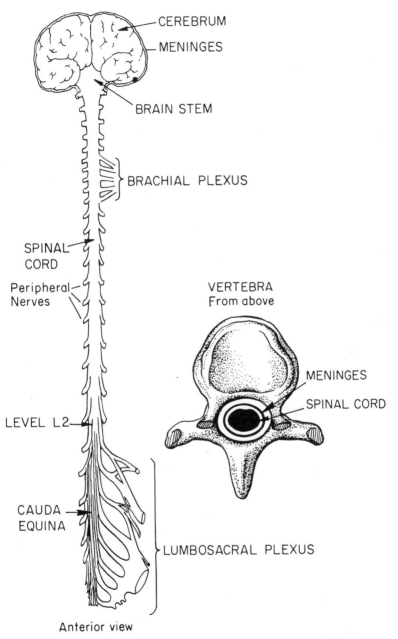

CEREBRUM

MENINGES

BRAIN STEM

BRACHIAL PLEXUS

SPINAL
CORD

Peripheral
Nerves

VERTEBRA
From above

MENINGES

SPINAL CORD

LEVEL L2

CAUDA
EQUINA

LUMBOSACRAL PLEXUS

Anterior view

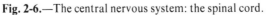

Fig. 2-6.—The central nervous system: the spinal cord.

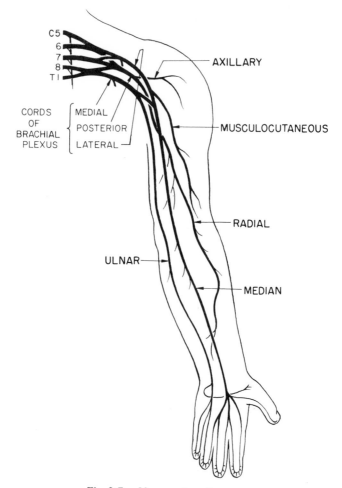

Fig. 2-7.—Upper extremity nerves.

median nerve and the *ulnar* nerve, both of which run down to the hand. The latter two supply the muscles that flex the wrist and fingers and so enable us to have a firm grip and make a fist (Fig. 2-7).

The nerves that go to the lower limbs form the *lumbosacral plexus*. The three major nerves given off by this plexus are the *femoral obturator* and *sciatic* nerves. The femoral nerve goes to the muscles that flex the hip and extend the knee. The obturator goes to the muscles for hip adduction. The very large sciatic nerve goes to the muscles that extend and abduct the hip, flex the knee, dorsiflex and plantar flex the ankle. At

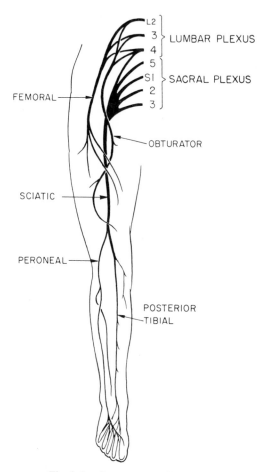

Fig. 2-8.—Lower extremity nerves.

the height of the knee, the nerve divides into the *peroneal* nerve, which goes to the muscles which dorsiflex the ankle, and the *posterior tibial* nerve, which supplies the plantar flexors of the ankle. From the function of this nerve one can see that a sciatic nerve injury causes severe impairment in walking (Fig. 2-8).

The Autonomic Nervous System

This part of the nervous system cannot be influenced by a person's own will. It is, therefore, involuntary.

The *autonomic nervous system* has two types of fibers, the *sympathetic* and the *parasympathetic* fibers. Each of these two forms of fibers causes a very specific effect on the various body organs. For instance, a stimulus from the parasympathetic nerves causes the heartbeat to slow, but a stimulus from the sympathetic fibers will speed up the heartbeat. If a person is nervous and excited, the sympathetic nerve becomes activated and the heartbeat increases. While the person is relaxed and asleep, the parasympathetic nerve takes over and slows the heartbeat down. The fibers of the autonomic nervous system travel along the peripheral nerves and the blood vessels and reach nearly every organ of the human body. Many of the essential daily bodily functions, such as digestion, urination and defecation, have a strong parasympathetic component.

The function and effect of the autonomic nervous system on the bodily organs is a manifold one. For the reader who desires more information excellent books on this subject are available.[1,2]

The general principle of sensory and motor pathways is the following: The origin of a nerve impulse can be traced to a sensory stimulus. This message is carried by sensory peripheral nerves to the spinal cord, where an ascending tract carries it to the brain. In the brain the sensation is noted and integrated. Now a response is formulated. The message of response is carried from the brain to a descending tract of the spinal cord and then to a motor peripheral nerve that makes the corresponding muscles contract. To a certain degree, all these responses are influenced by activity of the autonomic nervous system.

Excellent texts are available for the reader who would like to gain more insight into the physiologic functions of the various body systems.[3,4]

REFERENCES

1. Langley, L. L.: The Autonomic Nervous System, in *Review of Physiology* (3d ed.; New York: McGraw-Hill Book Company, Inc., 1971).
2. Guyton, A. C.: The Autonomic Nervous System, in *Basic Human Physiology* (Philadelphia: W. B. Saunders Company, 1971).
3. Shepheard, R. J.: *Alive Man; the Physiology of Physical Activity* (Springfield, Ill.: Charles C Thomas, Publisher, 1972).
4. Nordmark, M. T., and Rohweder, A. W.: *Scientific Foundations of Nursing* (2d ed.; Philadelphia: J. B. Lippincott Company, 1967).

CHAPTER **3**

MODALITIES FOR HEAT AND COLD

To prepare the muscles and joints of a body region for exercise therapy, various modalities for heating these structures are employed. Heat helps to reduce pain and tightness in the muscles and stiffness in the joints. In the body region in which the temperature is elevated, the blood vessels dilate and the blood flow increases. All these changes aid in the performance of exercise therapy. Such heat application has basically the same purpose as the warming-up and loosening-up exercises that are used by athletes just prior to entering a strenuous event.

Furthermore, heat can be applied to parts of the body by immersing them in heated water. This form of heating is termed *hydrotherapy* (Greek *hydor*, water). In hydrotherapy, the heat which is delivered to the immersed body parts is only one of the therapeutic factors from which the patient can derive benefit.

The aim in the use of heating modalities is to effect a temperature elevation and an increased blood flow in the part or region selected for therapy.

The optimal benefit from local heat application is usually reached in 20 minutes. After this time no further local temperature elevation can be achieved. The increased blood flow carries the heat away into the whole body.[3,4] *Remove metals or jewelry from the area to be treated.*

The various heating agents used in physical therapy can be divided into two forms: the one that brings heat to the superficial structures, and the one that brings heat to deeper structures of a body region.

Not only temperature increase, but also temperature decrease in selected body regions, is used therapeutically. The lowering of tissue temperature is achieved by ice application in various forms. It is used to decrease swelling, inflammation and spasticity.[1,2]

Superficial Heating Agents

To this group belong the modalities which can effect temperature elevation close to 10 mm under the skin surface.[5] Hydrocollator packs, infrared lamps and paraffin baths have these physical properties.

51

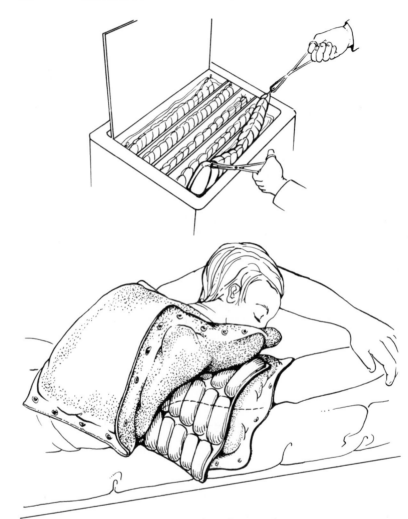

Fig. 3-1.—Hydrocollator packs.

Hydrocollator Packs

A hydrocollator pack (from Greek *hydor,* water, + Latin *colare,* to filter through, to permeate) consists of a silica gel encased in a canvas bag that can be contoured to the various body regions (Fig. 3-1). Silica gel maintains a temperature of 40 C (104 F) for 30–40 minutes. Such a hydrocollator pack is placed in a water bath with a temperature of 77 C (170 F). The pack has to be removed from the water bath and placed on the area that afterward will be treated with range-of-motion, active or resistive exercises. The body areas where these moist packs are applied, as well as the packs themselves, are covered with thick Turkish toweling to protect the skin from burns and to reduce emission of heat from the packs toward the outside. The upper side of the packs can also be covered with a plastic or rubber sheet to forestall heat emission away from the packs.

If there is a chance that the patient's heat and cold sensation is impaired, the patient's sensitivity should be tested first by the supervising physical therapist. This can be done easily by using small glass tubes as used in medical laboratories, one filled with hot water and one with cold water. Place each tube on the area where the packs will be applied. If the patient can feel that one glass tube is hot and one is cold, it is safe to assume that temperature sensation is intact. Impairment of temperature sensation occurs after nerve injuries and in diseases of the nervous system. Loss of heat sensation can lead to bad skin burns without the patient's experiencing any pain at all. Intact temperature sensation is important for application of superficial heating agents. If there is any question, the physician should be consulted for direction.

It is advisable to place these packs on the patient instead of having the patient lie on them. The latter invites greater chances for burns. Sometimes the patient's condition requires the placing of hydrocollator packs under a part of his body, however. Special precautions have to be taken, as instructed by the supervising physical therapist.

The heat delivered from the moist hydrocollator pack to the body is a conductive type of heat. The moisture of the pack serves as a conductor to the skin surface. Water is a good heat conductor. So are metals, mainly copper and silver. For example, when we heat one end of a copper wire, the other end, which is away from the heating source, becomes hot immediately. Wet or damp clothes do not preserve the body heat but conduct it to the outside, and the wearer feels cold and shivery. The counterpart of conductors are insulators, which hamper the transfer of heat, such as wood, asbestos, plastics and rubber. The rubber wet suit for swimming and diving in cold water preserves the heat generated by the body system.

If the patient suffers from a skin ailment, hydrocollator packs should not be used. The same is true for areas of impaired blood supply.

After 20 minutes the hydrocollator packs should be taken off and placed for reheating in the 77 C (170 F) water bath. Thirty minutes later the packs are again ready for application.

Infrared

This form of heat is found widely in nature and daily life. The most generous of all infrared sources is the sun. More than half of the sun's total radiation is infrared, and most heated substances emit infrared

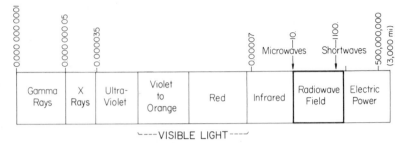

Wavelengths in Centimeters

Fig. 3-2.—Electromagnetic spectrum.

rays. A glowing belly stove and electrical light bulbs are examples. Infrared produces a comfortable, soothing, warm feeling on the skin. It is radiant heat and can so be transmitted to an object or the body from a distant source through a vacuum.

The physical properties of any radiant energy are that of electromagnetic waves. The spectrum of the electromagnetic waves ranges from electric power supply and radiowaves, with a very long wave length, through the visible light, to x-rays, with a very short wave length. The wave length of infrared is longer than that of visible light (Fig. 3-2).

For therapeutic purposes an artificial source is used for infrared radiation. The infrared lamp (Fig. 3-3) consists of a nonluminous wire core to which electric energy is applied. Infrared can effect temperature elevation down to 10 mm under the skin surface.[5]

The infrared source should be 30–50 cm from the body area to be treated. To assure optimal heat radiation effect, the infrared source should be placed perpendicular to the area that is to receive infrared rays. The surrounding body parts can be draped when infrared effect to these regions is not desirable. The infrared lamp has to be turned on 20–30 minutes prior to its use to achieve an adequate output of heat. A few moments after the beginning of the infrared heating, the skin exposed to it turns red and feels hot. The patient should be alerted to report the feeling of "hot spots" immediately. Such hot spots may be the initial warning signals of an imminent burn.

There are some practical advantages to infrared. There is no pressure on the body, and the technician attending the patient can easily observe the area without interrupting treatment.

As with other local heating methods, the optimal local temperature is achieved in approximately 20 minutes. Any extension of this time period leads to sweating and general heating. The effects of infrared are very similar to those of the heat emitted by hydrocollator packs. It also should not be applied over areas of impaired vascular supply or impaired temperature sensation.

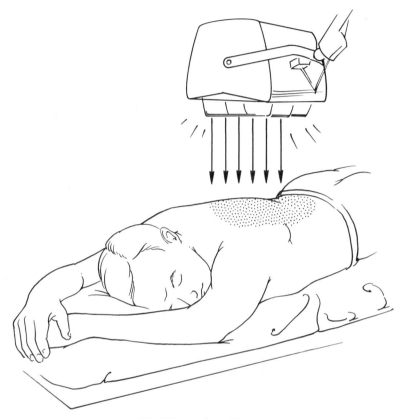

Fig. 3-3.—Infrared lamp.

Paraffin Bath

The paraffin bath (Fig. 3-4) contains a mixture of 1 part of liquid petrolatum to 7 parts of paraffin. After these components are placed in the container of the paraffin bath, the mixture has to be heated till the paraffin melts. Before it is ready for use, the temperature of the paraffin-petrolatum mixture has to drop to 51–54 C (125–130 F). A period of 2–3 hours may be required for this drop in temperature.

The paraffin bath is used to treat small areas like hands and feet. Arthritic joint pain and stiffness in the hands are a frequent indication for paraffin use. *Prior to paraffin application the skin should be cleaned and dried. Jewelry has to be removed.*

The patient has to be instructed to dip the hand quickly in and out of the paraffin 10–12 times. He must keep the fingers spread to allow the paraffin to form a glove. The paraffin glove is usually 7–12 mm in

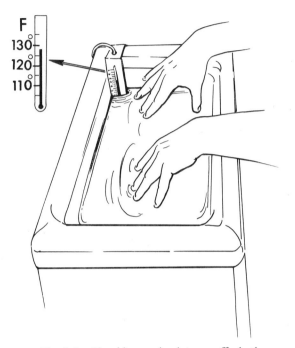

Fig. 3-4.—Hand immersion into paraffin bath.

thickness. The patient feels some glowing warmth and tingling in the fingers. The tingling is thought to be a result of the dilation of blood vessels brought on by the increased temperature. The heat that is emitted from the cooling off of the paraffin is brought to the body tissue by conduction. There is also some radiation of infrared from the solidifying paraffin.[6]

The finger's thickness is usually not much more than 10 mm. This explains how we can deliver heat inside the joints of the fingers, since heat is conducted from all directions to the fingers when they are coated with paraffin. The coated part should be covered with paper towels to diminish heat emission. Additional wrapping with a thick towel is advised. Underneath the paraffin glove, the vapor from the sweat of the heated hand forms a thin layer. This layer prevents the heated part from being burned. The paraffin layers can also be brushed on.

After the paraffin coat has been applied for 20 minutes, the patient has derived all possible benefits from this mode of heating. The paraffin glove is then removed. First it has to be loosened around the wrist and then rolled to the distant ends of the fingers, as we do when removing a tight rubber glove. The used paraffin can be placed again in the paraffin container.

To have paraffin ready for use all the time, the container should be connected with electricity and the thermostat set at 51–54 C (125–130 F). The paraffin-petrolatum mixture should be exchanged every 6–12 months.

The contraindications for paraffin use are the same as for use of hydrocollator packs. Paraffin must not be applied when there is evidence of skin infection, or an impairment of sensation or of the blood supply in the part to be treated.

Deep Heating Agents

This type of heating modality emits energy in the form of electromagnetic or mechanical waves. These waves have the physical properties to elevate the temperature of tissue as far down as 30–50 mm under the skin surface.[3,7] Electromagnetic waves generate heat by the tissue's resistance to electric current. Mechanical waves cause a form of tissue vibration that generates heat.

Deep heating by electromagnetic or mechanical waves is called *diathermy* (Greek *dias,* going through, + *thermos,* heat).

An analogue to the heating of tissue with electromagnetic waves is the warming up of a wire that conducts electric current. The amount of the generated heat depends on several factors and is governed by Joule's laws, which state:

A rise in temperature in a conductor is caused by the passage of an electric current. The degree of temperature rise is dependent on the amount of heat produced.

The amount of heat produced is:

a. Directly proportional to the resistance of the conductor in ohms.

b. Directly proportional to the square of the strength of the current in amperes.

c. Directly proportional to the length of time the current flows.

Deep heating, or diathermy by electromagnetic waves, is done by means of a microwave or a shortwave generator.

Microwaves

One of the more frequently used deep heating or diathermy machines is the so-called microwave diathermy machine (Fig. 3-5).

Microwaves are located on the right of infrared in the electromagnetic spectrum (see Fig. 3-2). The wave length is longer than that of infrared rays, but shorter than the wave length of electromagnetic waves, which can supply mechanical power. Microwaves are within the radio wave field frequency.

The microwave machine consists of a generator, which is operated by

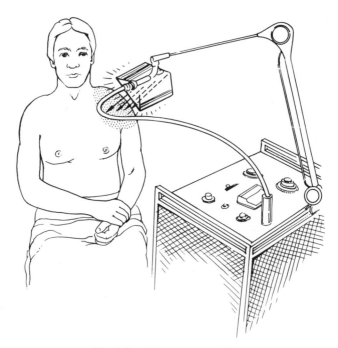

Fig. 3-5.—Microwave machine.

electrical power; the director, which emits the microwaves, and a spacing gauge. The microwave generator is a magnetron that generates high-frequency electric energy, the microwaves. No part of the microwave machine comes in contact with the patient.

The distancing of the director from the part of the body that is to be treated is of importance. It can be accomplished accurately by the spacing gauge. The director should be perpendicular to the treated body part. The intensity of the microwaves that reach the body part to be treated decreases with the square of the distance between the microwave director and the body part.

Prior to the use of microwaves one has to be certain that the skin of the area to be treated is clean and dry. Moisture and grease would increase the skin resistance, which could cause a burn. As with other heating agents, the optimal temperature elevation is obtained in 20 minutes.

Microwaves must not be applied if the patient has a cardiac pacemaker. The cardiac pacemaker, which is inserted under the patient's skin, sends out electric impulses to the heart to maintain a regular heartbeat. Microwaves could interfere with the function of such a pacemaker and lead to serious complications.

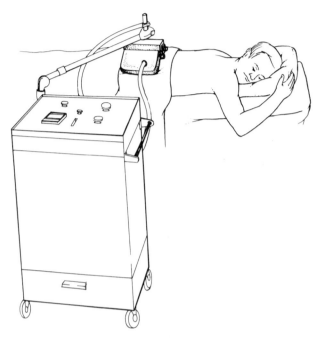

Fig. 3-6.—Shortwave diathermy machine.

One outstanding feature of microwave application is its potential to deliver heat accurately to a relatively small specific area. A temperature elevation up to 41 C (106 F) as deep as 30–50 mm under the skin surface can be achieved.[3,5]

Shortwaves

Another form of diathermy or deep heat application is the use of shortwaves. "Shortwaves" is a confusing term. The so-called shortwaves have a longer wave length than microwaves. In the electromagnetic spectrum (Fig. 3-2) they are located, therefore, to the right of the microwaves.

The term "shortwave" has a historical background. In the early years of diathermy by electromagnetic waves, longer wave lengths were used as compared with the more modern shortwave machines.

The shortwave diathermy machine (Fig. 3-6) consists of an electric power supply unit, an oscillator unit, a shortwave frequency circuit and a patient output circuit. The widely used household alternating current is transformed by the oscillator unit into electromagnetic waves with the length and frequency of shortwaves. The shortwaves are within the radio wave frequency range.

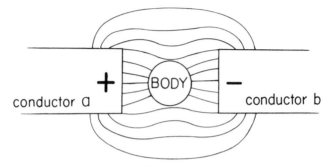

conductor a   conductor b

Fig. 3-7.—Electromagnetic field.

The application of shortwave diathermy is somewhat more difficult than microwave application. The shortwaves are delivered to the patient by contour applicators, inductance cable or air-spaced electrodes. The patient's skin is protected with a thick Turkish towel. The Turkish towel serves to absorb the sweat from the surface of the skin.

The body region to be treated should be within the electromagnetic field that is generated between the applicator devices (Fig. 3-7). A milliampere meter is located on the panel. It indicates the amount of energy that is "drained" by the body. At a certain meter reading it will indicate that the patient output circuit is tuned to the oscillator unit. This means maximal flow in the area to be treated.

In recent years the use of shortwave diathermy has decreased. It is more and more replaced by microwave therapy.

Contraindications for shortwave diathermy are the same as for microwaves. It must not be used in hemorrhage, acute inflammation or marked circulatory disorders and near metallic implants.

Ultrasound

Another deep heating treatment is ultrasonic wave application. Ultrasonic waves are not faster than sound, but of a higher frequency than the sound waves which can be perceived by the human ear. The principles of the ultrasound wave, which is a mechanical wave, are the following: Electricity is applied to a crystal of a certain physical constitution. This crystal in turn starts to emit ultrasonic waves, which penetrate the superficial tissue and are reflected on the deep tissue. This sets up a very fine vibrating motion in the tissue, which in turn generates heat. A similar effect is the heating up of a wire that is bent back and forth rapidly.

The principal difference between electromagnetic waves and ultrasound waves is that the latter are mechanical waves. The

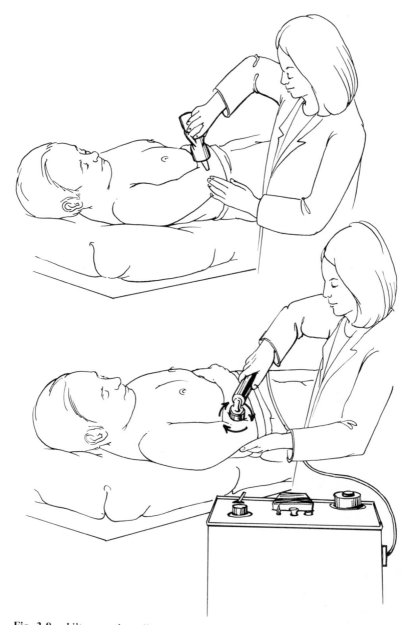

Fig. 3-8.—Ultrasound application: *above*, applying coupling agent; *below*, use of ultrasound head.

mechanical force of sound and ultrasound waves can be demonstrated by a membrane placed in the course of these waves. A vibrating motion takes place in the membrane. Ultrasound is transmitted by media that are not compressible, like water or mineral oil.

The application of electricity to a crystal that in turn emits mechanical waves is called the *reversed piezoelectric effect* (Greek *piezein*, to press).

The ultrasound machine (Fig. 3-8) contains a power supply and an oscillator circuit. The latter transmits the ultrasound waves generated in the crystal to the ultrasound head. The ultrasound head is moved in a stroking or circular motion over the part to be treated. These motions help to distribute the energy. A rule of thumb is to move the head about 10 cm/second. A commercially available coupling agent or mineral oil has to be applied. Ultrasound can also be applied under water. This method is sometimes used when irregular surfaces like hands or feet are treated. The energy output is usually set at 2 watts/cm.^{2}

The therapeutic application of ultrasound is very limited, but in recent years it has had great diagnostic use in heart and eye diseases.

Hydrotherapy

Whirlpool

The whirlpool (Fig. 3-9) consists of a container filled with water. By an agitator the water is brought into a whirling motion. This whirling motion has a massaging effect on the skin and tends to dilate the blood vessels. This massaging effect also soothes pain. The whirlpool is mostly used for joint complaints in wrists, ankles and knees, and after fractures.

The whirlpool temperature usually ranges from 37 to 40 C (98 to 104 F).

Much care should be exercised in adjusting the temperature of the whirlpool water. If the temperature is too high, this may be deleterious to the patient. Patients with peripheral vascular disease tolerate increased temperature poorly, since they have a reduced blood circulation that does not suffice to carry away excessive heat.

The whirlpool also is applied for 20 minutes. Exercise therapy can be used during and after whirlpool therapy.

Therapeutic Pool

The therapeutic pool is usually kept at a temperature of 37 C (98 F). It has an inclining bottom so that the patient can be brought into the deep side or into the shallow side.

This type of pool is mostly used for patients who have an affliction in

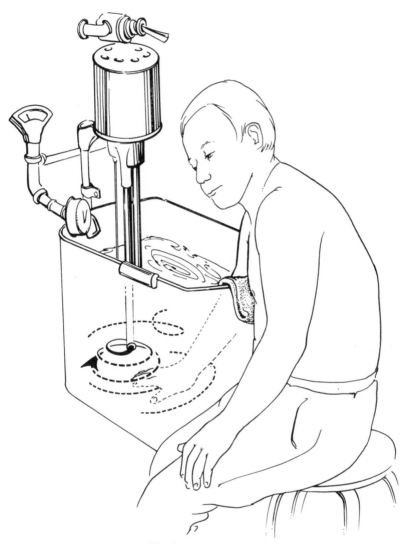

Fig. 3-9.—Whirlpool.

the lower extremities. It is used for gradually increasing ambulation after hip, knee and back surgery. There are other ailments of the musculoskeletal system in which exercise therapy in the pool has an ameliorating effect.

The patient is started with floating in the pool and standing in deep water, which, through its buoyancy, reduces the weight of the submerged body parts on his legs. Gradually he progresses to the shallow side, and as he goes to the shallow side the weight on the lower extremities increases.

Walking in the therapeutic pool also is helpful for strengthening the muscles of the lower extremities. To overcome the resistance of the water, increased muscle activity is required.

A pool is a very expedient mode of treating patients, but the same results can be obtained in rehabilitation departments without the use of a therapeutic pool. If a department does not have a therapeutic pool, this does not mean that its care is inferior.

Cold Therapy

Application of cold therapy is done with a large ice cube or a plastic pack of ice cubes frozen at 0 to −2 C (32–28 F).

The ice should be placed or rubbed over the area to be treated till the patient feels some numbness. The time this takes is usually 10–15 minutes. Shortly afterward a redness of the skin will appear, the so-called skin erythema. Exercise therapy should be initiated immediately afterward.

Cold therapy is frequently applied to reduce swelling, inflammation and spasticity.

It should be kept in mind that the use of heating or cooling modalities is an auxiliary measure. Application of a heat or cold modality by itself usually does not benefit the patient significantly. Heat or cold modalities are used as precursors of therapeutic programs such as exercises, gait training or stretching.

REFERENCES

1. Miglietta, O.: Electromyographic characteristics of clonus and the influence of cold, Arch. Phys. Med. 45:508, 1964.
2. Petajan, J. H., and Watts, N.: Effects of cooling on the triceps surae reflex, Am. J. Phys. Med. 41:240, 1962.
3. Worden, R. E., et al.: The heating effects of microwaves with and without ischemia, Arch. Phys. Med. 29:751, 1948.
4. Richardson, A. W., et al.: The relationship between deep tissue temperature and blood flow during electromagnetic irradiation, Arch. Phys. Med. 31:19, 1950.
5. Lehmann, J. F., et al.: Temperature distribution in the human thigh, produced by infrared, hot pack, and microwave application, Arch. Phys. Med. 47:291, 1966.
6. Mills, C. A.: Infrared Heat Transfer Principles—Application to Man, in Glaser, O.: Medical Physics (Chicago: Year Book Medical Publishers, Inc., 1960), vol. 3, pp. 299–302.
7. Lehmann, J. F., et al.: Comparative study of the efficiency of shortwave, microwave, and ultrasonic diathermy in heating of the hip joint, Arch. Phys. Med. 40:510, 1959.

CHAPTER **4**

THERAPEUTIC EXERCISES

One of the more difficult tasks for a physical therapy technician is to teach a patient an exercise program. Most of the time it does not suffice to show the patient just once how to do the exercises; the technician has to re-emphasize certain very specific details and has to correct the patient's performance frequently and adjust it to his physical condition at the particular time. Much effort and dedication on the part of the therapist and the therapy technician are often needed to improve the patient's performance. While each patient reacts differently to an exercise program and needs individual consideration in the program outline, there are well-established physiologic principles which should always be adhered to. Some of these principles are:

1. The purpose and goal of the exercise program have to be very clearly defined. For instance, it has to be decided whether the patient's general physical condition should be improved or whether the range of motion of a specific joint should be increased or a specific muscle be strengthened. The program has to be designed accordingly.

2. The amount of stress which the exercise program places on the patient in general or on a specific joint or muscle has to be determined according to the patient's tolerance and the strength of the specific muscle or the condition of the joint.

3. When an exercise program is designed, the type of stress imposed by the exercise must be relevant to the function which will be enhanced. For instance, extending the knee against resistance and gravity will strengthen the quadriceps muscle. There should be a steady attempt, day by day or week by week, to perform better. In other words, the tolerance of the patient or the strength of the muscle and the range of joint motion should be challenged steadily. If a person only performs the activity he is accustomed to, he will not increase his strength, tolerance or skill.

4. The program should adhere to well-established physiologic principles; that is, the intensity and duration of the stress imposed should increase gradually. To achieve an increase in strength and tolerance or endurance, the exercise program has to be performed, if not daily, at least at frequent, regular intervals. It has been observed by many workers in the field that increase in strength, endurance or physical skill

is not a straight uphill course. There are daily and sometimes weekly vacillations, and therefore the exercise program has to be adjusted accordingly.

5. Do not exhaust the patient. If he still feels fatigued the day following the exercise program, it was too strenuous for him and he has to be given a rest. The same applies to the specific muscle or joint which was exposed to exercise stress. Should the muscle be painful or weaker, or the joint more swollen and painful the day following the exercises, the program has to be eased temporarily.

Improvement is not entirely a physiologic function; psychologic factors do play a role. Many of the problems your patients are faced with are long-lasting and are therefore more apt to be the cause of discouragement. Many of the patients entrusted to your care will need much encouragement. Also remember that a substantial number of the patients you will encounter may have ailments that cannot be entirely cured—but, remember, the patient's functioning nearly always can be improved. The patient has to be made aware of this by his physician. This potential for improvement only, not complete cure, may sometimes dampen the patient's motivation to perform the prescribed program.

Various Forms of Exercises

The various forms of exercises are named according to the effect that they are designed to achieve.

Range-of-Motion Exercises

If a joint is not regularly moved, it becomes stiff, and the range of motion decreases. You may have noticed the desire to stretch after you have been lying in one position for a long time. With advancing age tightness and stiffness of the joints sets in more readily, and it becomes more difficult to restore normal range of motion. For instance, in a person who is unable to move one arm or leg after a stroke because no impulses can travel from the brain to the peripheral motor nerves, the joint's range of motion decreases, and the tissue around the joint contracts and shortens. In the case of a temporary or permanent paralysis, the treating person has to move the patient's limb through the ranges of motion. In this instance one speaks of *passive* range-of-motion exercises. If the person is able to move the limb by active muscle contractions, we speak of *active* range-of-motion exercises.

There are many other conditions, such as joint inflammation or trauma, that result in restricted joint motion. For instance, patients with Parkinson's disease (see Chapter 5), whose main feature is loss of voluntary motion and general stiffness (rigidity), also often suffer from restricted motion in the joints as a consequence of the movement disorder characteristic of the disease. Care must be taken to prevent such joint contractures by means of daily range-of-motion exercises and stretching. It is easier to prevent contractures than to restore normal range of motion after contractures occur. In most persons the daily activities, which usually consist of motions repeated many times in the course of a day, are sufficient to maintain the range of motion of the joints. At any time normal activity is impaired, either by a disease affecting the general health or by a process affecting joints, muscles, bones or nerves, measures should be taken to prevent joint contracture.

Range-of-motion exercises can be performed by a physical therapy technician after he is instructed in them by a physical therapist. The American Academy of Orthopaedic Surgeons has published a booklet that gives information about normal range of motion and technics for measuring and recording findings.[1]

Exercises to Increase Strength

Whenever a muscle or a group of muscles is forced into inactivity, the strength of those muscles gradually fades away. If total inactivity is forced upon a patient, the rate of decrease in muscle strength is about 7.5% per day.[2] The most visible feature that separates muscles designed for skilled and speedy motion from muscles designed for strength is the size of the muscle. This has been confirmed by many scientific investigations, and can be observed in the human or animal body. For instance, the muscles which are able to lift the body weight, like the quadriceps muscle in stair walking (see Chapter 9), or the gastrocnemius muscle (see Chapter 5), are large muscles. In contrast, the muscles that are designed to perform more skillful motions, such as the muscles of the thumb, are much smaller. If a person is very well trained for physical performance—a runner or competition swimmer, for example—the number of individual muscle fibers is not much higher than in the various corresponding muscles in the untrained person. The size of the individual muscle fiber is greater, however.

Muscles that are forced into inactivity become flabby and eventually decrease in size. In case the peripheral nerve or the so-called lower motor neuron is damaged and the muscle cannot contract at all for many months, the muscle fibers which cannot contract are replaced by nonfunctional fibrous tissue. In such situations, the muscle cannot be made stronger any more.

When a skeletal muscle contracts against gravity or resistance or both, the individual motor units necessary to effect a contraction come into action on a rotatory basis. This means that not all the motor units are recruited simultaneously for a contraction of the muscle to perform work. The individual motor units go in and out of action. When a contraction against gravity or resistance or both is maintained for approximately 5 seconds, nearly all of the motor units necessary to effect contraction and joint motion come into action within these 5 seconds at some point. The greater the resistance against contraction, the greater the challenge and the more motor units will be activated. The greater the load on the muscle, the more fibers are needed to effect a contraction.

The so-called *progressive resistive* exercises of DeLorme are designed to increase the strength of the muscles. The principle is that of repetitive maximal contraction against resistance, with the resistance gradually increasing. For instance, when the quadriceps muscle has to be strengthened, weight will be placed around the ankle or the foot. The knee will be brought into full extension, which will be maintained for 5 seconds, and then bent again. This motion should be repeated 10 times. As the strength of the muscle increases, weight or manual resistance should be increased. Many variations have been proposed since DeLorme publicized his method in 1945.[3] The original principle, however, has withstood the test of time and is still the most useful method for strengthening muscles. The resistance, in this instance the weight, should always be placed at the same distance from the joint line of the joint that the muscle to be strengthened will move. Remember your instructions in mechanics: The work load increases with the distance from the rotating point. Furthermore, the measurements of improvement in the muscle strength by increased ability to lift a certain number of kilos would be totally inaccurate if this distance were varied.

There is another form of exercise that helps to maintain, or perhaps even improve, the strength of a muscle. These are the so-called *static* or *isometric* exercises. "Isometric" (from Greek *isos,* equal, + Greek *metron,* measure, of, relating to or characterized by equality of measure) means that the muscle is contracted without bringing about any joint motion. Claims have been made that this form of isometric contraction, when performed several times daily, does increase strength. It was once thought that two or three contractions daily would suffice to maintain strength. This claim is not widely supported at this time. There is a very important practical value in isometric exercises, however. They can be used when active motion in the joint is not possible or desirable. For instance, isometric contractions of the quadriceps and gluteal muscles are frequently advised for patients who are bedridden. Isometric exercises are also sometimes used to facilitate active exercises. Out of fear of causing pain in an inflamed joint, the patient often thinks he is unable to contract a muscle, and sometimes it is necessary to show him that he is still able to do it.

There are various methods of measuring the strength of a muscle. It can be done with measuring devices or manually. Manual muscle testing is the more widely used method. To test the strength of a muscle adequately, the examiner has to have exact knowledge of the tested muscle's origin and insertion and the direction of its maximal force upon the joint. Correct positioning of the joint and the extremity whose muscle has to be tested is of utmost importance. Usually manual muscle testing is performed by an experienced physical therapist, but this skill can be acquired by a physical therapy technician if he wishes. An excellent text of manual muscle testing is available.[4]

The most widely used grading of muscle strength in manual muscle testing is as follows:

Normal—complete range of motion against gravity with full resistance

Good—complete range of motion against gravity with some resistance

Fair—complete range of motion against gravity

Poor—complete range of motion with gravity eliminated

Trace—evidence of slight contractility, no joint motion

Zero—no evidence of contractility

Grading becomes very difficult if the patient has an upper motor lesion and suffers from spasticity or rigidity. No adequate testing can be performed when contraction against resistance or even active motion causes pain.

Skill or Coordination Exercises

Every skilled motion, like tying shoelaces, writing or sketching, depends on the intact functioning of various components of the nervous system. The structures that conduct the sensory input, the structures in the brain that integrate the various stimuli in the cortex and the nerve tract that conducts the motor stimuli to the end organ, the skeletal muscle fibers, have to be intact. When we speak of improvement of skill, coordination and balance, we really mean that we increase the control which the individual has over various muscle contractions. To have a high degree of control over the various muscle groups takes many years of experience and practice. A very young child has the necessary reflexes, nerve structures and muscles to perform all the skills adults can perform so easily and so well; yet the child's movements appear clumsy, the gait is still broad-based and he falls more frequently than do adults. When a high degree of precision in muscle control is achieved, even strenuous motions appear very easy to the eye of the observer. For instance, an accomplished gymnast appears to be featherlight. Precision of control wanes somewhat in advanced age (see Chapter 5).

When a disease causes movement disorders, there is usually some loss of skill and coordination. Even when a person loses a limb, for instance a leg, there is usually some problem with balance (see Chapter 9). The artificial limb, regardless of how sophisticated and well-fitting it is, always lacks one component, the sensory input. The only sensory input is in the area where a well-fitting prosthetic socket is in contact with the skin of the stump. Prior to the loss of the limb, walking was an automatic activity; the person did not have to pay any specific attention to this activity. Now walking is a task that needs careful eye control and special attention by the patient. For instance, after a stroke the patient may have return of active motion in the involved arm or leg, but there may be a loss of sense of position. Therefore, the patient may have difficulties in performing skilled activities with the involved hand, in spite of having sufficient strength.

Various exercise programs are available in print for specific disease entities—for instance, the parkinsonian exercise program, which is designed to counteract the effect of the disease. As with the progressive resistive exercise programs, exercises to increase control of muscle action have to be performed, if not daily, at least very frequently. The challenge to improve muscle control has to be steadily increased, otherwise no improvement can be achieved and the patient stays at the same level of function.

In patients with injury to the central nervous system resulting in impairment of movement, often the so-called *proprioceptive neuromuscular facilitation patterns* are employed. This form of exercise is based on the neurophysiologic development of motions in infancy. The exact place of this form of exercise in rehabilitation is not yet established.

Special breathing exercises to increase air exchange to the lungs are often employed in patients who are afflicted with a lung disease or an ailment which diminishes the expansion of the rigid thoracic cage and, as a consequence, decreases air exchange to the lungs (see Chapter 2).

These specific exercises have to be directed by an experienced physical therapist. If the reader of this book wants to gain more information about these therapeutic exercises, there are excellent texts available.[3]

The learning of skills or, in other words, the acquisition of a better and more precise control of muscle action and muscle coordination, needs constant reinforcement by the person who treats the disabled.

Control of muscle action can be lost by long-standing disease as it is after a serious illness. In such instances, skill nearly to the same level as previously can be regained with training. It is always easier to retrain for previously acquired skills than to learn new skills.

When a part of the nervous structure has been permanently damaged, however, it is hardly possible for a patient to be retrained to the same level of precise muscle contraction control that he possessed prior to the injury. With much effort the patient can improve in control to such a degree that he can perform the activities of daily living without the help of another person. For instance, a patient may not regain sufficient control to shave with a razor blade, as he did prior to the damage; he may, however, regain enough skill to shave with an electric shaver.

Many elderly people cannot walk because some insult to a part of the central nervous system has offset their balance. Despite excellent rehabilitation therapy, control of balance may not be regained to the degree it was present prior to the insult that injured the central nervous system. However, the patient can be trained in a certain form of gait and can become acquainted with the use of a walking aid. This will enable him to walk safely again and to function in his environment without the help of another person.

REFERENCES

1. *Joint Motion: Method of Measuring and Recording* (Chicago: American Academy of Orthopaedic Surgeons, 1965).
2. Hettinger, T., and Mueller, E. A.: Muscular strength and muscular training, Arbeitsphysiologie 15:111, 1953.
3. Kottke, F. J.: Therapeutic Exercise, in Krusen, F. H., Kottke, F. J., and Ellwood, P. M. (eds.): *Handbook of Physical Medicine and Rehabilitation* (2d ed.; Philadelphia: W. B. Saunders Company, 1971).
4. Kendall, H. O., Kendall, F. P., and Wadsworth, G. E.: *Muscles: Testing and Function* (2d ed.; Baltimore: Williams & Wilkins Company, 1971).

CHAPTER 5

GAIT AND GAIT DEVIATIONS

An understanding of the normal human gait provides the basis for the treatment and management of gait deviations that occur in persons with impairment of the function of the lower extremities.

The human gait is the result of a series of rhythmic alternating movements of the arms and legs and the trunk. These various movements create a forward motion of the body. They mainly occur between legs, pelvis and spine, as well as between arms, shoulders and spine. A person walking at a speed to which he is accustomed swings the arm and shoulder forward as the leg of the other side is brought forward. The same phase relationship between arms and legs is present in running. The extent of the movement is greater, however.

There is a slight difference in the walking pattern of any one person as compared to another. One can recognize a good friend at a great distance by his gait particularities. One can also recognize a long-time friend by the characteristic sound his footsteps make without having him in sight. Differences in the walking pattern are relatively small; the principal pattern is the same for all individuals. These individual particularities of the walking pattern do not mature till about age 7–9.[1] Before this age, the youngster's body experiments to find the best pattern for his body build.

The Normal Gait

The normal gait cycle consists of two major phases, the *stance phase* and the *swing phase*. The *gait cycle* is the time interval between successive heel strikes of the same foot. The stance phase begins when the heel of the shoe of one extremity strikes the floor; it ends when the toes of the same foot leave the ground. The swing phase begins with lifting the toes off the floor and ends when the heel again strikes the ground after the leg has been brought forward. About 70% of the gait cycle time is taken up by the stance phase and the remaining 30% by the swing phase.

The stance phase (Fig. 5-1) consists of the following components: the *heel strike,* when the heel contacts the floor; the *midstance,* when the sole of the foot is flat on the ground and the body weight is directly over

Heel Strike   Midstance   Toe Push-off

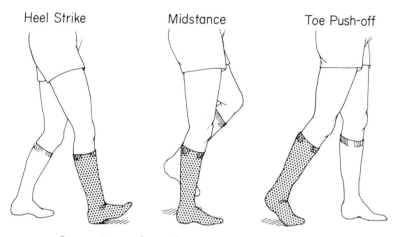

Stance Phase (Rt. leg) ‑70% of Gait Cycle Time

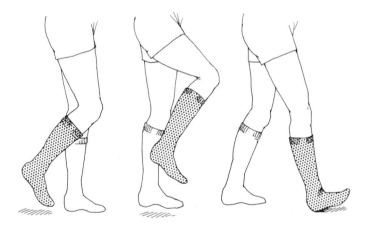

Swing Phase (Rt. leg)‑ 30% of Gait Cycle Time

Fig. 5-1.—Normal gait.

the stance-phase leg, and the *toe push-off*, when the heel of the stance-phase leg rises from the floor and the body is pushed forward by the ball of the foot that is still in contact with the ground. At this moment, the body is propelled forward by the forceful action of the calf muscles and hyperextension of the hip.

The stance phase terminates and the swing phase begins when the entire foot rises from the ground. During the swing phase, the leg must be accelerated to get in front of the body, ready for the next heel strike. To clear the ground in the swing phase, the leg has to be shortened by hip and knee flexion. The leg is now brought in front of the body and in front of the leg of the other side. The swing phase ends at the moment of the heel strike. At this moment the distance between the heels is approximately 50–70 cm. The distance varies with the individual gait particularities and the age of the person.

There is also a rotation of the pelvis around the spine in the horizontal plane (Fig. 5-2). The rotation is usually 6–8 degrees. The pelvis

Fig. 5-2.—Pelvis rotation in normal gait.

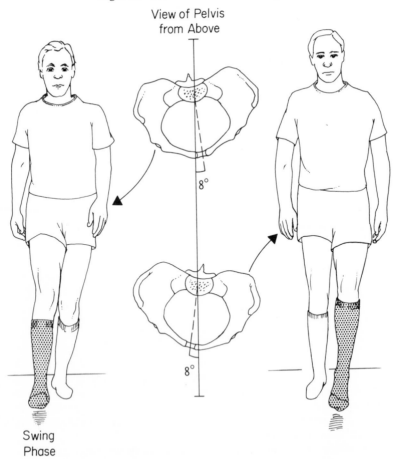

View of Pelvis
from Above

8°

8°

Swing
Phase

starts to rotate forward 6–8 degrees at the beginning of the swing phase. The rotation comes to a stop at the time of the heel strike. As full weight is placed on the leg in midstance phase, the rotation of the pelvis in the horizontal plane is reversed. As the leg of the other side goes into the swing phase, the pelvis on that side starts to rotate forward.

The shoulder girdle moves in the horizontal plane with the same degree of excursion as the pelvis, but the shoulder moves in reversed order. On the side where the pelvis rotates forward, the shoulder rotates backward.

At one point of the gait cycle there is a period of double support when the 2 extremities are in contact with the ground simultaneously. This double support occurs between toe push-off on one side and heel strike and midstance phase on the other side. The length of time of double support is directly related to the speed of walking: As the walking speed decreases, the length of time spent in double support increases. As speed increases, double support decreases; and as the person changes from walking to running, double support disappears.

In running, the toe push-off on one leg is completed before the heel strike of the other leg. Therefore, at some point of the gait cycle, both legs are in the air during running. The fact that both legs are without ground contact at some moment is the main feature which separates running from walking.

In old age, a decreased elasticity of the ligaments and muscles and some loss of smoothness of the joint surfaces bring some change in the gait. Changes in the neurologic system also contribute to gait alterations. In old age, the gait loses the appearance of being effortless. The step becomes shorter and wider. The frequent need among the elderly to use a cane resembles to some degree the holding on to a firm object during a child's first attempts at walking. Certain diseases of the nervous and skeletomuscular system, prevalent among the older age population, cause very characteristic gait deviations. One such ailment, frequently found among the elderly, is osteoarthritis of the hip joint, which results in the painful-hip, or *coxalgic,* gait (from latin *coxa,* hip, + Greek *algos,* pain).

The Painful-Hip Gait (Coxalgic Gait)

In osteoarthritis of the hip, the smoothness of the head of the femur is replaced by unevenness. The motion of the hip joint, that is, the motion of the femoral head in the acetabulum, is hampered by increased friction and becomes restricted and painful. In swing phase, when hip and knee have to be flexed to bring the leg forward and in front of the other foot, flexion of the hip joint may be painful and restricted. The hyperextension of the hip at the end of the stance phase may be diminished.

With hip flexion and hyperextension reduced, the step becomes shorter. To enable the swing-phase leg to clear the ground in very severe restriction of hip flexion, the stance-phase leg goes up on the toes (Fig. 5-3). The width of the step is reduced, depending on the degree of abduction limitation. The gait found in osteoarthritis of the hip with only mild hip joint restriction appears nearly normal to the untrained eye, due to the flexibility of the lumbar vertebral spine. The flexibility of the lumbar spine also enables patients with osteoarthritis of the hip to sit in a chair and climb stairs normally.[2]

When there is pain in the hip joint on only one side, the weight-bearing period on the painful side is shorter than on the normal side (Fig. 5-4). The person tries to shorten the burden of weight on the painful hip as much as possible. Therefore, the stance phase becomes shorter and the swing phase longer on the painful side. Just prior to the weight-bearing period, that is, when the weight-bearing leg goes into midstance phase, the trunk shifts laterally to the painful side. The purpose of this lateral shift is to bring the line of gravity of the trunk closer to the weight-bearing painful hip joint. The closer the line of gravity to the weight-bearing hip, the less forceful a contraction of the hip abductor muscles is required to keep the pelvis horizontal. The more

Fig. 5-3.—Gait in restriction of left hip motion.

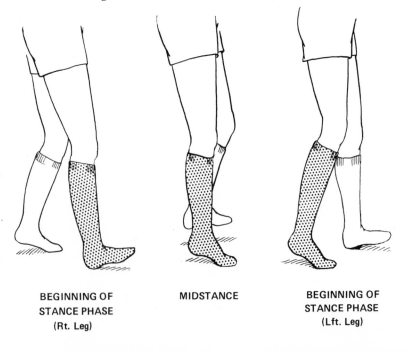

BEGINNING OF
STANCE PHASE
(Rt. Leg)

MIDSTANCE

BEGINNING OF
STANCE PHASE
(Lft. Leg)

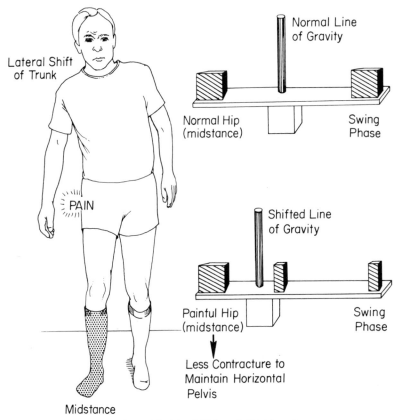

Fig. 5-4.—Weight shift in painful-hip gait.

forceful the contraction of the abductor muscles, the more stress is placed on the hip joint, and the more pain is caused in the arthritic hip.

The components of the normal gait that may be increased in the painful-hip or coxalgic gait are flexion and extension of the lumbar spine, and with it the backward and forward tilting of the pelvis. The lateral shift of the trunk is also often increased, mainly in one-sided hip pain. The cadence (from Latin *cadere,* to fall; the beat or measure of any rhythmic motion or activity, as marching, dancing, rowing; number of steps per minute) may be diminished.

The Painful-Knee Gait

A stiff or painful knee is not infrequent in old age. This may be due to osteoarthritis or other forms of joint affliction. Flexion and extension of the knee becomes painful. To protect the knee, the patient contracts the

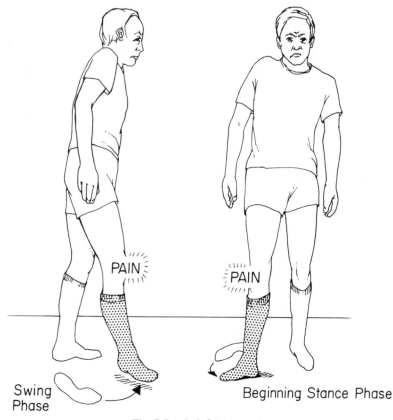

PAIN

PAIN

Swing
Phase

Beginning Stance Phase

Fig. 5-5.—Painful-knee gait.

quadriceps to suppress any motion in the knee. This alone does not
protect the knee sufficiently, however, when the leg is in stance phase.
The patient therefore assumes an outward rotation of the affected limb
(Fig. 5-5). The medial aspect of the knee and foot are pointed in the direction of forward motion. Thus, all flexion and extension play in the
knee is avoided, and the whole sole can be placed on the ground. There
is no heel-to-toe motion. This outward rotation of the affected limb cannot be assumed by external rotation in the hip alone. There is also some
increased rotation of the pelvis. The pelvis is rotated forward on the
affected side, and backward on the unaffected side. Therefore, there is
an internal rotation of the hip on the unaffected side. The step with the
affected leg is shortened in length, and the stance or weight-bearing period is very short since weight-bearing produces pain. The step is

widened because flexion of the hip without flexion of the knee carries the leg outward.

The gait is similar in cases of a painful affliction in one of the joints of the great toe.

The Sacroiliac Gait

During normal gait, there is a motion between the sacrum and the iliac bone. Both bones are connected firmly with ligaments. These connections, however, allow some motion during walking. With increasing age, this motion becomes more difficult because of increased friction and loss of elasticity of the ligaments. Also, osteoarthritic changes of the bone may contribute to the loss of motion. Persons who have an affliction in the sacroiliac joint walk slightly bent forward and with decreased motion of the pelvis. The gait has the appearance of being very cautious and does not have the features of complete relaxation that a normal gait shows. Pain in the sacroiliac region leads to a slight shortening of the step because there is no movement between sacrum and iliac bone.

The Flexed-Hip Gait

This type of gait is assumed by persons who suffer from flexion contractures of the hip joint capsule. Hip flexion contracture is frequently found in patients who are confined to long periods of sitting because of pain in the lower extremities. The pain does not necessarily have to be caused by an affliction of the hip joint. Persons who are bedridden for long periods of time also often develop flexion contractures of the hip. The primary disease process is not necessarily in the hip joint.

When both hips are flexed, there is a forward bending of the trunk during all phases of walking (Fig. 5-6). The posterior limitation of the hip motion in extension causes a flexion of the trunk when the hip should be hyperextended at the end of the stance phase. The flexion of the trunk is a compensation for the loss of hip extension. The total length of the step is shortened on both sides because neither hip can compensate for the loss of hyperextension at the end of the stance phase by increased flexion in the swing phase. With hyperextension lost, the toe push-off at the end of the stance phase is not so forceful as in persons with normal hips. The forward tilting of the pelvis at the end of the stance phase is increased, but it cannot sufficiently compensate for the loss of hyperextension in the hip.

In hip joint disease, and in any other condition that causes limitation of motion in the hips, it is mostly flexion and extension that become

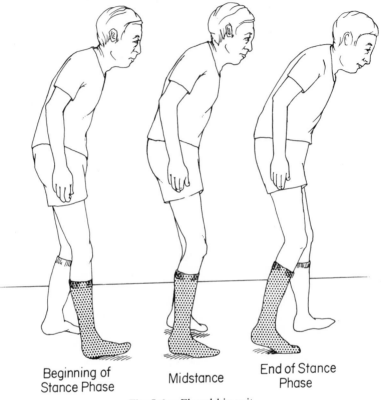

Beginning of
Stance Phase   Midstance   End of Stance
Phase

Fig. 5-6.—Flexed-hip gait.

limited very quickly. Occasionally, there is also a limitation of internal and external rotation. In these instances, the horizontal rotation of the pelvis is also decreased because of limitation in the motion of the femoral head in the acetabulum. With the rotation of the pelvic girdle decreased, comparable motion of the shoulder girdle decreases also. Oscillation of the center of gravity is minimal, since the trunk is bent forward in all phases of walking, and the push-off at the end of the stance phase is diminished.

Hip flexion contractures are very disabling, and all efforts have to be exerted to prevent such contractures. Some of the methods used to minimize them in ambulatory and bedridden patients are: the use of high seats such as those used by draftsmen; range-of-motion exercises and passive stretching, and avoidance of painful stimuli.

The Hemiplegic Gait

A gait deviation found mostly in elderly persons is that caused by neurologic involvement in a stroke. It is the so-called *hemiplegic* gait.

The patient has loss of motion in the arm and leg on one side. Four to 6 weeks after the onset of the stroke, spasticity often sets in. The loss or partial loss of motion and the onset of spasticity result in a rather severe gait deviation. When the hemiplegia is on the right side, the arm swing on the right is lost. The patient has the arm dangling if it is flaccid, or in a flexed-elbow position if spasticity has set in. The motion of the leg in swing phase depends on several factors. Again, at the stage when spasticity has set in, the patient is unable to bend his knee in swing phase. In addition, there is loss of ankle dorsiflexion. To clear the ground in swing phase, the hip has to be abducted and the trunk flexed to the healthy side to gain some elevation, or hiking up, of the pelvis on the affected side (Fig. 5-7). At the beginning of the stance phase there is no heel strike; the patient walks on the outside of his affected foot. In cases of heel-cord contracture, the patient, in midstance phase, may find support only on his toes and metatarsal bones. The heel may never touch the ground. When the affected leg is in swing phase, the patient pushes himself up on the healthy side by elevation of the heel. The transfer of the involved leg from backward to forward in swing phase is not a smooth motion but a rapid and jerky one. The patient actually throws the leg forward. In a flaccid as well as in a spastic hemiparesis, it is the toes and not the heel that touch the ground first at the beginning of the stance phase. The trunk does not straighten up completely, but stays bent forward. This places the center of gravity in front of the knee to avoid buckling of the knee. Depending on the degree of spasticity in the involved leg, there are variations in the various components of the gait cycle.

Gait in Parkinson's Disease

Another disease of the central nervous system that causes a characteristic gait deviation is parkinsonism. This ailment can now be ameliorated by drug therapy. It occurs mostly in the older population.

The patient stands with a slightly forward-flexed trunk and flexed knees and hips (Fig. 5-8). Sometimes there is also a continuous tremor. The base of the step is somewhat widened. When walking, there is no arm swing. The trunk oscillates from the right to the left in a block. In the vertical view, there is no rotation between the pelvic or shoulder girdle and the spine. The legs are advanced rigidly and with hesitation. The swing-phase heel does not pass the toes of the other leg, which is in stance phase. If we take the footprints of a patient with a parkinsonian

End of Stance Phase   Swing Phase   Beginning of Stance Phase   Swing Phase

Fig. 5-7.—Hemiplegic gait.

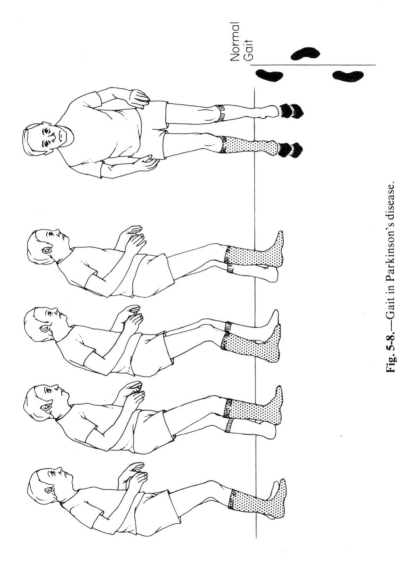

Normal Gait

Fig. 5-8.—Gait in Parkinson's disease.

gait, we find the steps in contact with one another from heel to toe. The angle of the foot to the forward line of progression is slightly less than normal. The severity of the gait deviation depends on the severity of the disease.

REFERENCES

1. Inman, V. T.: Human locomotion, Canad. M. A. J. 94:1047, 1966.
2. Murray, M. P., Gore, D. R., and Clarkson, B. H.: Walking patterns of patients with unilateral hip pain due to osteoarthritis and avascular necrosis, J. Bone & Joint Surg. 53A:259, 1971.

CHAPTER 6

TRANSFERS AND BODY MECHANICS

As early as possible during recovery from some disabling condition, or despite a permanent loss of function, patients need to be as active and as independent as possible.

One of the basic abilities for a physically disabled person, and fundamental to his independence, is the ability to move from one place to another—for instance, getting out of bed into a wheelchair, getting from the wheelchair onto the toilet or getting from a wheelchair into a car. Because these tasks involve moving the weight of the body against gravity, they can be very difficult for any weak or paralyzed patient. The process of moving from one surface to another is called a *transfer*.

While the severely disabled patient may need to have someone actually lift or slide him from one place to another, an important part of a transfer is that the patient must exert all the effort of which he is capable. The efforts of a moderately disabled person may still not be enough to move him to where he wants to go. He is not lifted, since the way for him to develop the ability to transfer is to keep attempting it. An assistant adds his efforts to the patient's, blocking him where he is unstable and assisting him where he is weak.

Knowing how to assist patients to transfer safely and efficiently comes from an understanding of *body mechanics*. This shows you how to position and move your trunk, legs and arms for the best leverage with the least stress and fatigue. Both you and the patient should move in ways that take advantage of gravity and momentum.

Exhibitions of applied body mechanics can be seen daily in a physical therapy department. There physical therapists, who are often young, graceful women, bring partially paralyzed patients often double their weight from a sitting into a standing position, or move them from bed to wheelchair. During a day's duty, physical therapists may have to do these maneuvers quite often. They have acquired the skill of positioning their bodies in relationship to the patient who has to be transferred in a mechanically advantageous way and have learned to avoid stress on certain parts of the body liable to injury, such as the back.

Before a patient is taught to transfer, the physical therapist or occupational therapist has carefully evaluated his abilities and weaknesses. The therapist takes into account the patient's general condition, his muscle strength and joint range of motion, his coordination and balance, his ability to understand and cooperate and any special condition such as non-weight bearing or decubiti. The therapist will decide the form of maneuver the patient should start to learn and will begin to work on this with him. At the same time, the therapist will begin an exercise program designed to strengthen the patient's weak areas and develop his abilities.

Evaluation will be a continuous process throughout the patient's treatment. As he is seen to respond, his program will be modified to correspond to his new abilities and new needs. The physician and therapist will decide on and designate a specific maneuver or exercise to the physical therapy technician, which he in turn should perform with the patient.

Only after the therapist and you yourself are sure that you are well in command of the various maneuvers should you perform them with the patient.

Forms of Transfer

There are two basic forms of transfer—standing and sitting. In a standing transfer the patient takes weight on one or both legs and comes to an upright position before sitting down again in the new place. In a sitting transfer the patient does not rise but moves his hips sideways from one surface to another, usually by taking the weight through his arms. Sitting transfers are used by people who cannot stand, such as patients with both legs paralyzed or amputated. They are also used for severely disabled patients who cannot assist in the transfer procedure.

Before beginning any transfer you should observe the following points:

1. Check the equipment and its position. It has to be stable and firm. If the bed has casters, they should be locked, or the bed should be pushed against a wall. The wheelchair must have its brakes locked and should, under some circumstances, be blocked against a wall.

2. The transfer surfaces should have the same height. A hospital bed can be lowered to the height of the wheelchair; placing a raised seat on the toilet can bring it up to the height of the wheelchair seat. Keep the transfer surfaces as close together as possible. Removable armrests and swing-away detachable footrests on the wheelchair will allow it to be positioned close to the bed or toilet. A sliding board, that is, a thin board placed across the two surfaces over which the patient slides, will close the gap between them completely.

3. The equipment should be positioned according to the patient's disability. The patient with one side stronger than the other, such as the hemiplegic, will usually prefer to move toward his stronger side in the

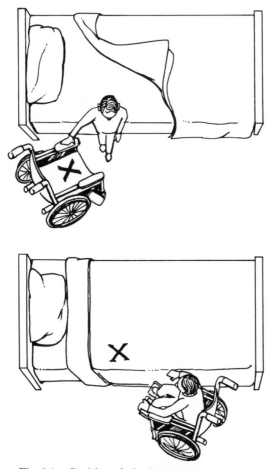

Fig. 6-1.—Position of wheelchair relative to bed.

transfer. If the wheelchair faces the foot of the bed when such a patient transfers out of the bed to his wheelchair, then the wheelchair will need to face the head of the bed when the patient wants to return to bed (Fig. 6-1).

4. The patient should wear shoes that fit snugly and have low, wide heels. The physical therapy technician also should wear shoes like this, with soles that will not slip. In case the patient has been prescribed a brace, it has to be applied prior to transfer.

5. The patient has to know what he is expected to do in the transfer. If he is forgetful or appears confused, he should be taught the process

one step at a time. Instructions should be simple—"Sit up," "Lock the brakes"—repeated when necessary and consistent from one time to another. Do not hurry the patient; allow him time to complete each step.

Place yourself in the right position for assistance to the patient and for safety for both of you during the transfer.

1. Stand close to the patient. If you stand apart from him, the strain on your back is greater. Stand with a broad base of support. Keep your feet apart, one foot ahead of the other. This position affords you good balance and allows you to shift your weight easily. If you keep your legs together, you may lose balance and fall with the patient. The patient may not only be injured, but he also will lose confidence in you. Do not play tug-of-war with him. Explain every motion to the patient. His efforts and your assistance have to be synergetic.

2. Assist the patient at the waist. Do not hold him at the shoulder. A transfer belt can be securely fastened around the waist of the patient.

Fig. 6-2.—Lifting with transfer belt.

This gives you a good grip on him without restricting his use of his arms (Fig. 6-2).

3. Keep your back straight, but have your hips and knees bent. Straighten your legs as you help the patient into the standing position. Lifting with the legs is much less strenuous to you than lifting with the back muscles. Let the patient see the surface to which he is transferring. Do not obscure his vision. A patient may become frightened if he cannot see the place he is going to.

Some patients, mostly the elderly, may not be in control of their urinary function, either temporarily after surgery, or because of some permanent impairment of the neurologic system. A catheter is then inserted through the urethra into the urinary bladder. It is frequently called an "indwelling catheter" or a "Foley catheter." The catheter is attached to a plastic bag that collects the urine. The bag is fastened to the patient's thigh or to the wheelchair. Whenever a patient transfers or gets out of his wheelchair, you must take care that this urinary catheter is not caught or pulled on. This could cause an injury of the tissue in the urethra, which, in turn, can lead to an infection in the urinary tract. Such an infection would increase or prolong the patient's disability.

The exact manner in which any patient will transfer depends on his abilities, the environment and many other circumstances. The following gives a step-by-step account of transfer procedures and suggests some variations. As you work with patients under the therapist's guidance, you will learn other ways.

Standing Transfers

Unassisted, Bed to Wheelchair

A patient with generalized weakness will go through the following motions to transfer unassisted from bed to wheelchair:

1. The patient slides forward to sit on the edge of the bed and puts his feet on the floor, with the stronger leg slightly behind and apart from the weaker leg. Then he leans forward (Fig. 6-3, *A*).

2. He stands by pushing down with his arms and straightening his legs.

3. After he stands, he reaches for support to the far-side armrest of the wheelchair. He pivots or steps to turn his back to the wheelchair (Fig. 6-3, *B*).

4. He bends forward to improve leverage and balance and slowly lowers himself to sit by bending his hips and knees and easing himself down while supporting himself with his hands on the armrests (Fig. 6-3, *C*).

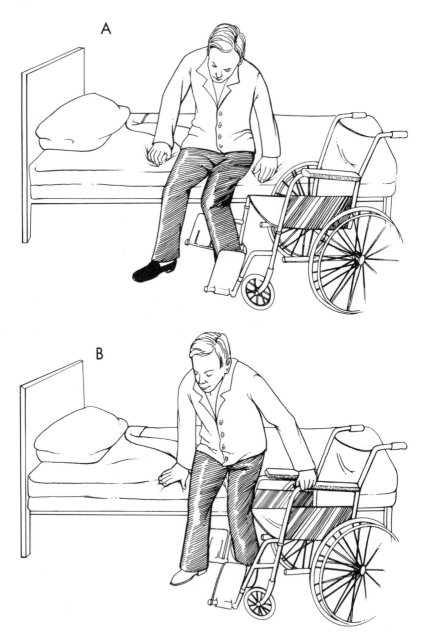

Fig. 6-3.—A and **B,** unassisted standing transfer from bed to wheelchair. (*Continued.*)

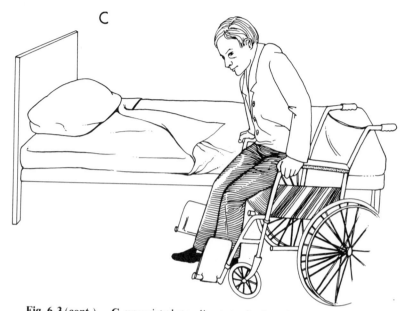

Fig. 6-3 (cont.).—C, unassisted standing transfer from bed to wheelchair.

Assisted, Bed to Wheelchair

If the patient does not have sufficient strength to bring himself from the lying into the sitting position, the assistance of a skilled person becomes necessary.

1. Keeping her back straight and her feet apart, the physical therapy technician bends hips and knees to become more level with the patient. She takes hold of the transfer belt or grips the patient around the waist with one hand and under the thighs with the other hand, thus assisting him to come into the sitting position at the edge of the bed. The patient may also need help in positioning the hands and feet (Fig. 6-4, *A*).

2. The physical therapy technician, while bending her hips and knees, places her feet so that she has a broad base and her knees block the patient's knees. She lifts the patient by the waist or by the belt as she straightens her hips and knees, and thus rises with the patient into the standing position (Fig. 6-4, *B*). The person assisting must keep slightly to the side to give the patient room to move and enable him to see the area he has to transfer to.

3. The physical therapy technician stands close to the patient, making sure that she still has a broad base of support and, if necessary, that her knees continue supporting the patient's knees. The patient and

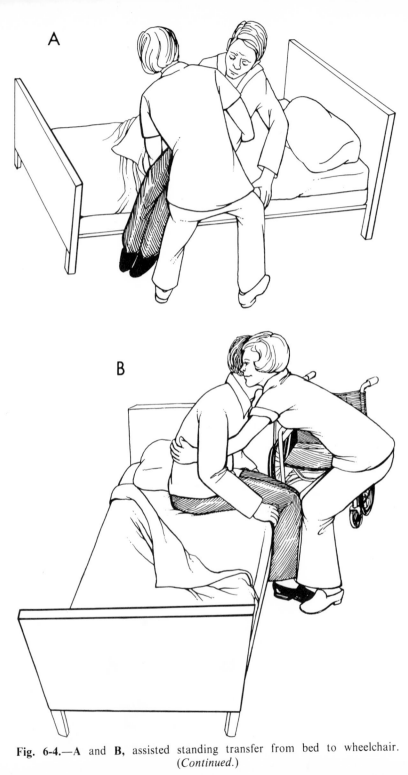

Fig. 6-4.—**A** and **B,** assisted standing transfer from bed to wheelchair. (*Continued.*)

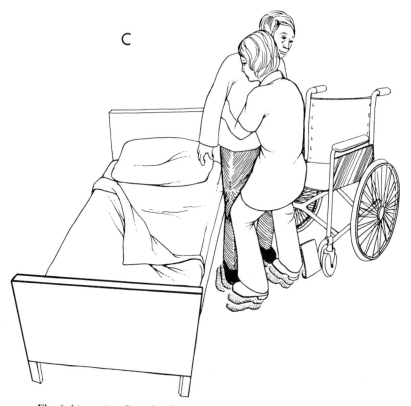

Fig. 6-4 (cont.).—C, assisted standing transfer from bed to wheelchair.

the assisting person pivot or turn together, shifting the weight from side to side and taking tiny steps (Fig. 6-4, *C*).

4. As the patient bends forward to sit, the assisting person slowly bends hips and knees, easing the patient to the seat and helping him in sliding back into the chair.

Assisted, Wheelchair to Parallel Bars

When the patient comes from the wheelchair to a standing position in the parallel bars, he has to bring the wheelchair as close as possible to the front end of the bars. The wheelchair brakes are then applied and the footrests swung aside. The patient moves to the front edge of the wheelchair or is assisted to do so. He has his feet flat on the ground and under his hips. The patient places his hands on the bars (Fig. 6-5). The technician bends hips and knees to bring herself to the patient's level,

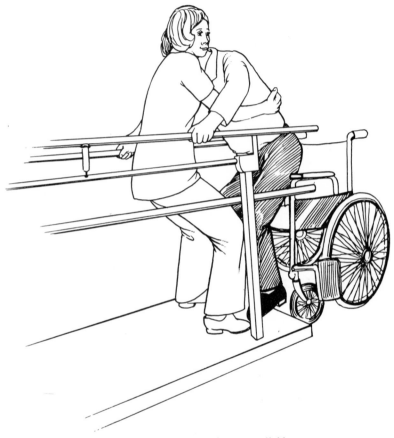

Fig. 6-5.—Assisted transfer to parallel bars.

blocks his knees and, lifting on his belt or waist, she and the patient rise together.

Assisted, Wheelchair to Treatment Table

When a patient has to be brought onto the treatment table, a stool with 4 rubber-tipped legs is placed near the table. The wheelchair has to be placed sideways to the treatment table, with the patient's stronger side near the table.

If the patient has one weak leg, the physical therapy technician blocks it with her knee while the patient steps up onto the stool with his strong leg (Fig. 6-6). The technician now blocks the strong knee as the patient lifts himself with the stronger leg, helped by the technician as she holds him around the waist or by the transfer belt. The technician

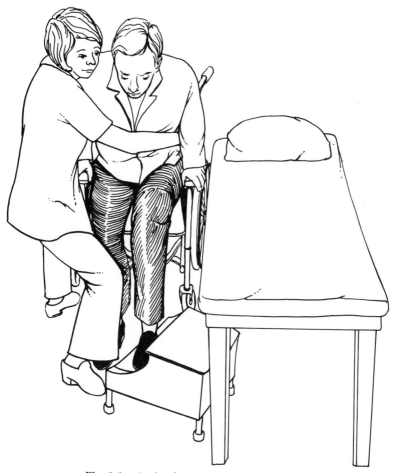

Fig. 6-6.—Assisted transfer to treatment table.

now turns the patient with his back toward the treatment table and helps him into the sitting position.

The stool usually is not needed in getting off the table. The patient will move to the edge, slide down onto his feet and then proceed with the basic transfer.

Modified Standing Transfer

Depending on the patient's specific disability, some variations of the transfer technics are required. For instance, with a hemiplegic patient whose arm and leg on 1 side are totally or partially paralyzed, the

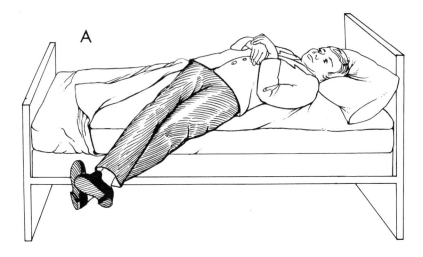

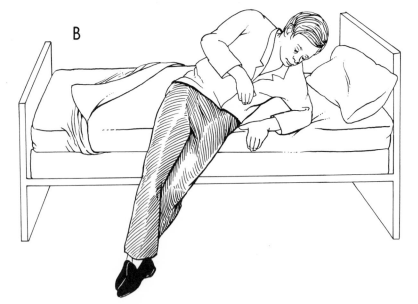

Fig. 6-7.—**A** and **B,** modified standing transfer of a hemiplegic. (*Continued.*)

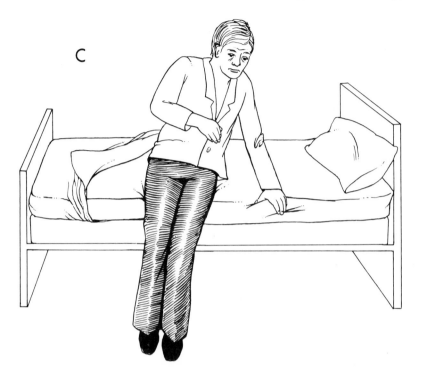

Fig. 6-7 (cont.).—C, modified standing transfer of a hemiplegic.

technician has to proceed in the following manner (in this example, the weak or nonfunctional side is assumed to be the right one):

1. To sit up in bed, the patient moves toward his left side.

2. He grips his weak right arm with his strong left hand and places it across the abdomen.

3. He pushes his left foot under the knee of the weak right leg. Then he slides his good foot down under the calf to the ankle. Crossing the ankles, so that the involved extremity can be supported by the normal one, he lifts or slides both legs over the edge of the bed (Fig. 6-7, A).

4. He holds onto the edge of the mattress with his left hand and bends his head forward. He keeps his head forward and leans with his weight against the left forearm and left elbow as he brings the left leg to the floor (Fig. 6-7, B). He then pushes on his left forearm and comes into the sitting position while straightening the left elbow (Fig. 6-7, C).

The remaining maneuvers necessary to complete the transfer into the wheelchair do not differ significantly from other standing transfers described earlier in this chapter.

The sequence of the various steps is reversed when the patient lies down in bed.

Standing Toilet Transfer

The same minimum locomotion potentials that are required for a standing transfer from bed to wheelchair are necessary for a standing transfer from wheelchair to toilet. The patient has to have one good leg, one good arm with a hand able to grip firmly and a good sitting balance.

Bathrooms vary greatly in size and arrangement of fixtures. The patient may practice with the hospital facilities, but the transfer method finally developed must be suitable for his bathroom at home.

Preferably, the toilet seat is 50 cm above the floor. Should the toilet bowl be lower than 50 cm, a raised toilet seat, which is readily available, can be fastened to the bowl without any difficulty (Fig. 6-8).

A 45-degree angle wall handrail should be placed on the wall that is closest to the side of the toilet bowl. The normal or stronger extremities should be on the side of the handrail when the patient is seated on the toilet. The rail is mounted on the wall at a 45-degree angle, with the lower part of the bar placed 5 cm behind the front edge of the toilet. The length of the bar may vary from 50 to 90 cm. The lowest part is near the toilet and should be approximately 90–95 cm above the floor (Fig. 6-9).

Fig. 6-8.—Raised toilet seat.

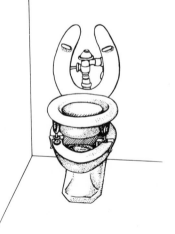

Fig. 6-9.—45-degree angle wall handrail.

Instead of a 45-degree angle wall handrail, a right-angle handrail can be installed. The horizontal bar is fixed to the wall behind the toilet bowl, and the upright bar is fixed on the floor 40 cm in front of the toilet seat. This bar should be only 75–80 cm above the floor and for short persons should be even lower than 70 cm. When using the right-angle handrail, the patient has to push downward with the hand to come to a standing position (Fig. 6-10).

With an oblique wall handrail, the patient has to pull himself into a

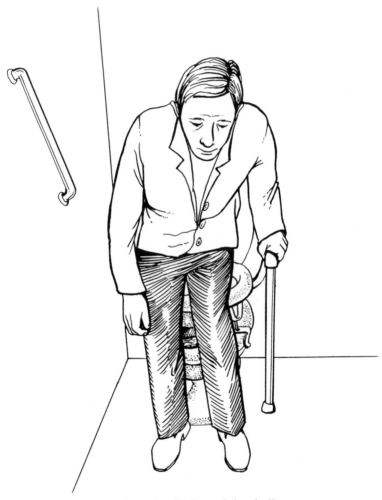

Fig. 6-10.—Right-angle handrail.

standing position. To enable the patient to push with an optimal
leverage, the right-angle bar has to be somewhat lower than the lowest
point of the oblique bar. Depending on the location of the toilet bowl in
the bathroom and on the side of the involved arm, either an oblique or a
right-angle handrail should be installed. For instance, if the toilet bowl
is close to the right wall of the bathroom and the patient's right arm is
impaired, a right-angle handrail would have to be installed on the left
side of the toilet bowl.

In preparation for the wheelchair-to-toilet transfer, the wheelchair has to be brought close to the front edge of the toilet. The patient's normal or stronger side has to be the nearest one to the toilet. Now the wheelchair has to be locked and the feet removed from the footrests, which have to be swung outward to the side or removed. The patient has to grip the handrail firmly and pull himself into the standing position (Fig. 6-11). The body weight should be borne entirely or mostly by the stronger leg. The trunk should be bent forward during this motion to have the center of gravity closer to the grip on the bar.

Fig. 6-11.—Standing transfer, wheelchair to toilet.

In case a right-angle bar has been installed, the patient has to push himself into the standing position. Should the leg which bears most of the weight have good hip and knee extensors, less pull on the handrail or less push with the hand is necessary to come into standing position. While the patient pivots on the good leg to turn the back toward the toilet seat, the grip on the handrail has to be maintained.

If a patient with a right hemiplegia has to transfer from the wheelchair to the toilet, he must bring his wheelchair as close as possible to the side of the toilet. Before rising to transfer to the toilet, he has to push down his slacks and underwear over the hips and move to the front edge of the wheelchair. He then pushes down with his left hand on the armrest of the wheelchair to help himself stand. Once erect, he reaches for the 45-degree angle wall bar or to the right-angle floor bar near the toilet bowl for support while turning his back to the toilet. If necessary, he may lean against the wall. He holds onto the bar to let himself down and to help himself up again.

Loosely fitting pull-on slacks and underclothes are easiest for the patient to manage. Some patients may need assistance with their clothing.

Standing Car Transfer

Patients with disabled or paralyzed lower extremities are nowadays able to drive a car with an automatic transmission. Such a car is equipped with hand controls. With the aid of these, the patient can apply brakes and accelerate the car with his hands. A special permit from the state bureau of motor vehicles is necessary.

The car transfer is an advanced, somewhat more difficult mode of transfer and can be accomplished unassisted only by patients with rather strong upper extremities and good body control.

1. Regardless of whether the patient is the driver or a passenger, he should always enter the car through the right front door. The steering wheel on the left side frequently hampers transfer. In addition, even if the patient is a passenger, the rear doors of the car may not open wide enough to allow proper positioning of the wheelchair for the transfer.

2. The door should be opened as wide as possible. For support, the patient may use the edge of the door after the window has been rolled down, the back of the car seat, the doorframe of the car or the seat of the wheelchair.

3. The patient turns his back to the car seat and sits down. He swivels on the seat to bring both feet inside, lifting up his involved leg with his hands if necessary.

4. To leave the car, the patient brings his feet firmly onto the ground outside the car before trying to stand up (Fig. 6-12).

Fig. 6-12.—Standing transfer, wheelchair to car.

When the car seat is very low, the patient may need assistance to get in and out of the car.

Bathtub Transfers

To get from a wheelchair into a bathtub by a standing transfer is one of the more difficult hurdles for a disabled person. The patient needs good balance and sure footing. A patient who can perform a standing transfer from wheelchair to bed may not be able to use this form of transfer to go from the wheelchair into the bathtub. He may have to use a sliding or a sliding-board transfer to diminish the risk of falling. The unusual feature of the bathtub transfer is that, contrary to other transfers, it is usually made toward the weak side. The reason is that it is much easier to get into the bathtub than to get out of it. Therefore, when the patient returns from the bathtub to the wheelchair, he can move with his better side first. There are some exceptions, however. For some patients it is easier to start the transfer into the bathtub with the good leg first, and they feel safer. Patients should have the opportunity of trying both methods.

To facilitate the somewhat difficult bathtub transfer, one sturdy chair of the same height as the bathtub edge should be placed inside the tub and one beside it. The chair which is placed in the tub should have rubber tips on the legs to avoid any slipping, which would jeopardize the patient's safety. A tread tape should be placed under the bath mat in the bathtub to avoid any slipping of the mat. Bars on the walls or attached

Fig. 6-13.—Bathtub with chair and mat.

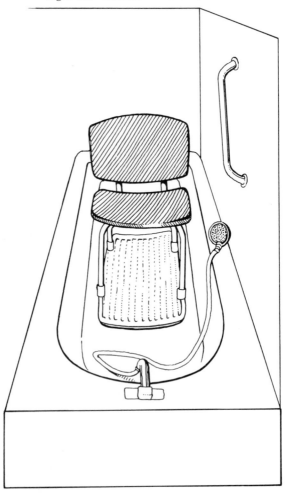

to the rim of the bathtub for the patient to hold onto are necessary (Fig. 6-13). In addition, a shower hose should be attached to the water faucet. After the patient assumes the sitting position on the chair in the bathtub, he can use the shower hose with the good arm.

Sometimes it may be difficult to place the proper chair beside the bathtub in the bathroom. The patient may also have some difficulties in sliding across the chair and the edge of the bathtub onto the chair in the bathtub. Under such circumstances it may be easier to teach the patient

Fig. 6-14.—Sliding-board transfer, wheelchair to bathtub.

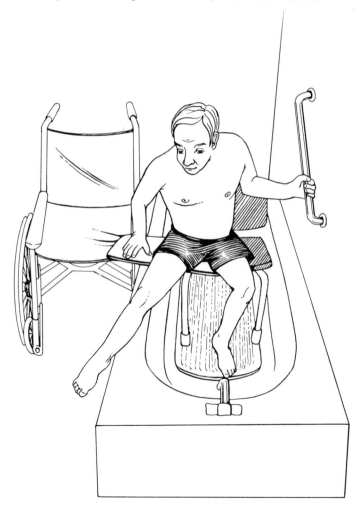

a sliding-board transfer. In addition, when disabled persons travel, it is easier to include a sliding board than a chair in the travel luggage. Also, in cases where the patient depends on chairs with certain specifications for transfer into the bathtub, it is safer to use the sliding board. The patient cannot be certain of having these specific chairs available at the place he travels to.

The sliding board consists of a lightweight pine board, 2 cm thick in the middle and beveled lengthwise to 1 cm at both ends. The length is between 60 and 80 cm, as needed, and the width is usually 22–30 cm. A width of 30 cm is required for very large persons only. The board has to be very smooth, and it has to be varnished or shellaced to prevent moisture entering the wood. The beveling makes sliding easier.

For the sliding transfer, the wheelchair is brought as close as possible to the bathtub. The wheelchair has to be locked, and the footrest and sidearm at the transfer side have to be removed. One end of the board is now placed securely under one side of the patient's buttock on the wheelchair seat and the other end on the chair in the bathtub (Fig. 6-14). Pushing down on the board with one hand and with the other hand on the wheelchair seat, the patient slides over to the edge of the bathtub and places the leg closest to the bathtub into it. Then he grips the hand-rail on the edge of the bathtub and slides his buttock onto the chair in the bathtub. He then brings the second leg over the edge of the bathtub.

Sitting Transfers

Patients who have weakness or paralysis in both legs and are unable to support their body weight with the legs, even for only a few seconds, have to transfer in a sitting position.

Unassisted, Bed to Wheelchair

When the patient is moving unassisted from bed to wheelchair, the wheelchair is against the bed sideways. The armrest and the footrest of the wheelchair that are near the bed have been removed, and the brakes are locked.

1. By leaning forward and pushing down with the fists into the mattress, the patient shifts his hips little by little until these are angled toward the wheelchair. With the arm closest to the wheelchair he now supports himself on the wheelchair seat.

2. Still leaning forward, he pushes down forcefully with one arm on the bed and the other arm on the wheelchair seat and slides his buttocks little by little from one surface to another. As he shifts position, he adjusts his legs. He must avoid pushing on the backrest of the wheelchair for support in transferring (Fig. 6-15).

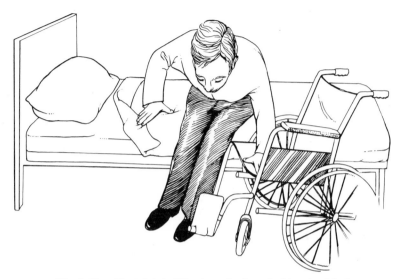

Fig. 6-15.—Unassisted sitting transfer from bed to wheelchair.

Fig. 6-16.—Assisted sitting transfer from bed to wheelchair.

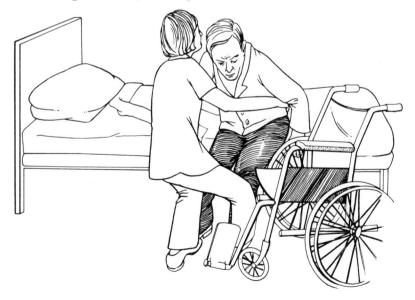

Fig. 6-17.—Draw sheet transfer.

3. He replaces the armrest, and pushing down on it with his hands, slides back into the chair and adjusts his legs with his arms, if necessary.

Assisted, Bed to Wheelchair

When the patient's arms are not strong and he cannot lift his body with his shoulder depressor muscles, he must be assisted in moving from bed to wheelchair.

1. The physical therapy technician bends her hips and knees to lower herself to the level of the patient. She grips the transfer belt or holds the patient around the waist and assists him in angling his hips toward the wheelchair. She also supports the patient's knees with her knees to prevent him from sliding forward.

2. Again, using the transfer belt or the grip around the waist, she assists him in sliding his buttocks to the wheelchair while allowing him to see the surface toward which he is transferring. Throughout the transfer, the physical therapy technician must allow the patient to lean forward so he can maintain his trunk balance (Fig. 6-16).

3. To help the patient move back into the chair, she pushes her knees against his knees, as the patient keeps leaning forward and pushes down on the armrests with his hands.

The same principles of body mechanics that are applied for a sitting transfer from bed to wheelchair, unassisted or assisted, apply to sitting transfers from wheelchair to toilet or wheelchair to car.

Draw Sheet Transfer

In case a patient is totally paralyzed or weakened to such a degree that he cannot participate in transfer at all, transfer from one surface to another is best done with a draw sheet. The patient is rolled to one side, and a folded sheet is placed under his back. The patient then is rolled to the other side, and the sheet is spread. Two persons, one on each side, hold the sheet and slide the patient, who is lying on his back, from bed to stretcher or treatment table (Fig. 6-17).

The degree of disability caused by a disease process varies from patient to patient. Some variations in transfer methods may be necessary, therefore.[1-3] The more variations the physical therapy technician is familiar with, the better she will be able to serve patients.

REFERENCES

1. Flaherty, P. T., Jurkovich, S. J., and Lundberg, A.: *Transfers for Patients with Acute and Chronic Conditions,* American Rehabilitation Foundation,

Rehabilitation Publication No. 702 (Minneapolis, Minn.: American Rehabilitation Foundation, 1970).
2. Lawton, E. B.: *Activities of Daily Living for Physical Rehabilitation* (New York: McGraw-Hill Book Company, Inc., 1963).
3. Peszczynski, M., and Fowles, B. H.: *Home Evaluations* (Cleveland, Ohio: Highland View Cuyahoga County Hospital, 1957).

CHAPTER **7**

HIP AND KNEE OPERATIONS

Arthritis of the Hip

Some of the more frequent joint diseases in the elderly population are arthritic afflictions of the hip. These afflictions diminish the range of motion, cause severe pain on weight bearing and make it difficult to walk on stairs, get up from chairs, put on socks and perform other activities of daily living.

Some of the patients who suffer from arthritis of the weight-bearing joints can now be helped with surgery.

Prior to 1940 the only forms of treatment available for degenerative arthritis of the hip were immobilization by plaster cast, bed rest or non-weight bearing on the side of the diseased hip. These forms of therapy were not very effective, and some of the elderly became wheelchair-bound and bedridden. Many of them were otherwise in good health and spirits and were expected to enjoy many years of active life. It was severe pain in the hip upon walking that crippled these patients.

Since 1940, *intertrochanteric osteotomy* of the upper end of the femur has been performed to alter the weight distribution of the damaged joint. One of the better-known operations of this type is the McMurray displacement osteotomy (from Greek *osteon,* bone, + Greek *temnein,* to cut). The thighbone is cut between the greater and lesser trochanter. The parts are repositioned and fixed by a plate (Fig. 7-1). This transfers most of the weight bearing from a damaged part of the femoral head to another, uninvolved part. For relief of pain, this form of osteotomy is still performed frequently, and many patients benefit from it.

Sometimes an *arthrodesis* (from Greek *arthron,* joint, + Greek *desis,* binding), that is, a fusion of the hip joint, is performed. After this operation, motion between the acetabulum—the concave part of the hip joint—and the femoral head is eliminated. Metal fixation with a hip nail is necessary to maintain the fusion. This operation is performed when the patient has a one-sided hip involvement only, and engages in vigorous physical activities. Vitallium cups or other artificial prosthetic inserts may not be equal to the stress a patient engaging in vigorous physical activity places on his hip.

111

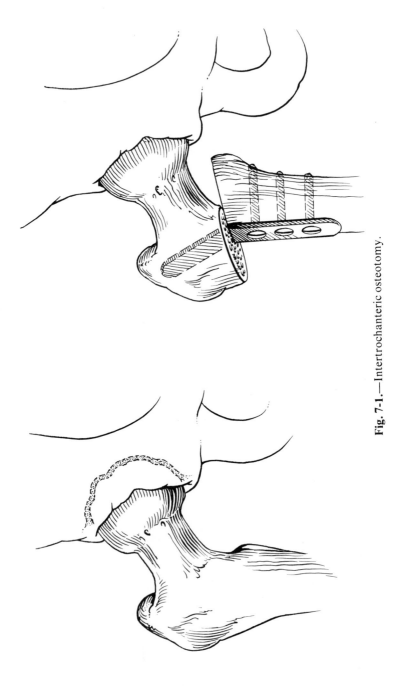

Fig. 7-1.—Intertrochanteric osteotomy.

Also, *excision arthroplasties* are done; that is, the head and neck of the femur are excised, which results in a mobile, painless, but very unstable hip. The removal of the head and neck of the femur decreases the pressure of the hip abductors and adductors across the hip joint.

Contraction of the hip abductor muscle increases the pain in the arthritic hip joint. To eliminate strong contractions in painful hips, a walking aid, as described in Chapter 8, is used. Furthermore, there is also a change in the gait pattern to diminish the contraction of the hip muscles on the painful side. This gait change is described in Chapter 5.

Another operation which relieves pain caused by pressure of the muscles on the arthritic hip is a surgical release of hip abductor, hip adductor and iliopsoas muscles.

Both operations, the resection of the head and neck of the femur and the release of the hip muscles, are now usually replaced by *cup arthroplasty*. The diseased surface of the femoral head is smoothened and covered with a Vitallium cup (Fig. 7-2). Cup arthroplasty plays an important role in the contemporary management of hip disease.

In recent years, surgery has mostly been directed toward replacement of the femoral head by plastic or metal prostheses. The plastic pros-

Fig. 7-2.—Cup arthroplasty.

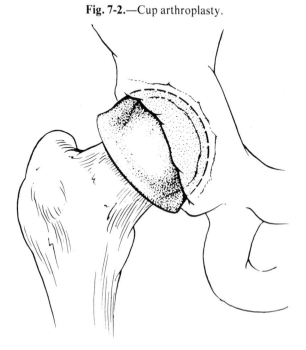

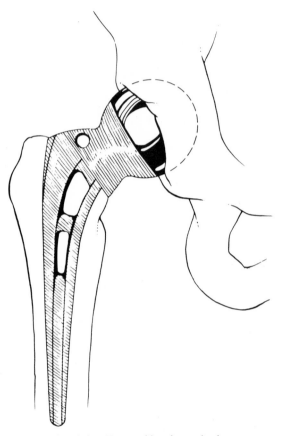

Fig. 7-3.—Femoral head prosthesis.

thesis was the so-called Judet prosthesis, and the metal one the so-called Austin-Moore or Thompson prosthesis (Fig. 7-3). The replacement prosthesis is driven into the shaft of the femur after the head and neck have been removed surgically. The damaged acetabulum is not amenable to treatment. The surgeon tries to make the surface as smooth as possible.

For many years, orthopedic surgeons have been aware that a complete hip joint with an artificial acetabulum, femoral neck and head is required to improve the fate of patients with severe arthritic affliction of one or both hip joints strikingly. Many trials were undertaken, but no lasting fixation of the artificial acetabulum to the pelvic bone could be achieved with screws. Finally, in 1958, the British orthopedic surgeons Charnley, McKee and Watson-Farrar succeeded in applying an

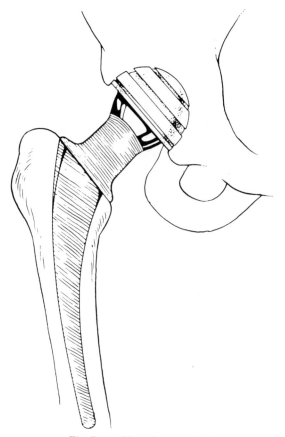

Fig. 7-4.—Charnley prosthesis.

artificial hip joint that provided lasting stability. Instead of screws, previously used for fixation, these surgeons used the cementlike synthetic substance methyl methacrylate. This is a polymer that is self-curing and results in a hardened mass.[1]

At the present time, the most frequently used artificial joints for total hip replacement are the Charnley and the McKee-Farrar prostheses.[2] The Charnley prosthesis has a femoral neck and head made of metal, while the artificial acetabulum consists of a high-density polyethylene plastic (Fig. 7-4). In the McKee-Farrar total hip replacement prosthesis, all parts, the acetabulum and the femoral neck and head, are made of metal (Fig. 7-5). The frequency of postoperative complications is now much reduced but, in spite of the most meticulous aseptic tech

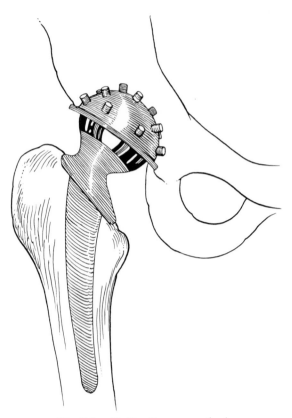

Fig. 7-5.—McKee-Farrar prosthesis.

nics in the operating room, infection in the bone at the site of insertion of the artificial parts is still a problem.[3] At the present time, however, the benefits outweigh the risk by far when the insertion of an artificial hip joint is indicated.

Hip Fractures

Besides patients who suffer from hip joint disease, the physical therapy technician who works in a general hospital, rehabilitation center or nursing home will also encounter a number of elderly people who had to undergo an operation on the hip because they fell and broke the thighbone near the hip joint. This form of fracture is generally referred to as "hip fracture." Older people are more likely to fall than younger people, because of decreased agility. In addition, their bones

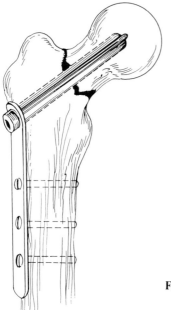

Fig. 7-6.—Smith-Peterson nail and plate.

are more brittle and break more easily. Prior to the use of metal nail and fixation plate, a broken hip meant bed rest for many months and often the application of a spica cast, which made ambulation impossible. Many of the patients succumbed to pneumonia, and many had to use two axillary crutches for the rest of their lives.

The American orthopedic surgeon Smith-Peterson was one of the first to use nail and plate to stabilize the fracture fragments immediately after the fracture had occurred. The internal fixation device now carries his name and is referred to as the Smith-Peterson nail (Fig. 7-6). It is still used for internal fixation of fractures of the femoral neck.

Basically, there are two main types of hip fracture: femoral neck fracture and intertrochanteric fracture.

Femoral Neck Fracture

The fracture line occurs through the femoral neck (Fig. 7-7, *A*). When the fracture line is very close to the femoral head, we speak of a *subcapital* fracture (Fig. 7-7, *B*).

Femoral neck fractures occur as frequently as intertrochanteric fractures (Fig. 7-7, *C*). Surgical management of the former is more difficult, however. The blood supply to the femoral neck is not as rich as that to

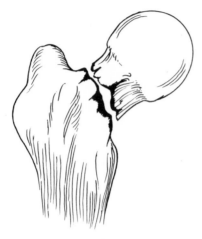

A. Neck of Femur

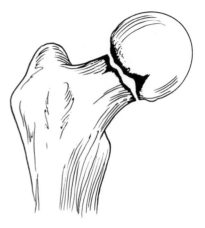

B. Subcapital

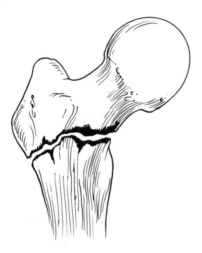

C. Intertrochanteric

Fig. 7-7.—Hip fractures.

other areas of the femur. This may lead to nonunion or to degenerative changes in the femoral head.

A number of internal fixation devices have been introduced to foster healing and allow early ambulation. One of these devices is the previously mentioned Smith-Peterson nail. Later on, the Knowles pins (Fig. 7-8) were introduced.

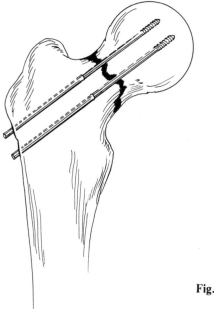

Fig. 7-8.—Knowles pins.

When the fractured femoral neck heals, there is always some degree of collapse of its bony structure and therefore some shortening. All metal fixation devices are therefore so designed that when these bony changes set in, the nail backs out and does not perforate the femoral head and the hip joint.

Sometimes aseptic necrosis may occur in the femoral head after fixation of a fracture with a nail, due to the impaired blood supply. This condition may require the surgical removal of the femoral head and neck and the use of a replacement prosthesis. Such devices have previously been described in this chapter.

The type of internal fixation used depends upon many factors. The surgeon in charge of the patient considers all these various factors and decides which mode of fixation or replacement is best for the particular patient.

Intertrochanteric Fractures

Intertrochanteric fractures usually tend to heal well because of the good blood supply, in contrast to femoral neck fractures.

Intertrochanteric fractures are commonly divided into the noncomminuted type (Fig. 7-7, *C*) and the comminuted type. By "noncom-

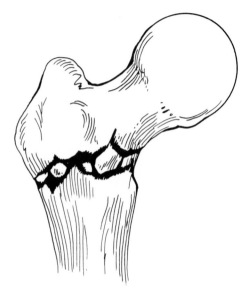

Fig. 7-9.—Comminuted intertrochanteric fracture.

Fig. 7-10.—Jewett nail.

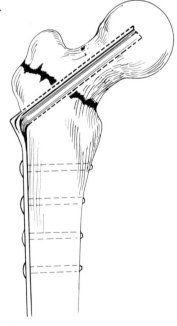

minuted" we mean that there is only 1 fracture line and a distal and a proximal fracture fragment. In a *comminuted* (Latin *comminutus*, from *com-*, together, + *minuere*, to diminish; thus, broken or crushed into small pieces) intertrochanteric fracture, there is more than 1 fracture line, and there are more than 2 bony fragments in the intertrochanteric region (Fig. 7-9).

To decrease pain and enable early ambulation, these fractures are fixed with metal nails and plates. The plate is affixed with screws to the side of the femur to control the nail that goes up inside the neck of the femur. The most frequently used device is the Jewett nail (Fig. 7-10). Several other devices with particular mechanical properties are available for the surgeon's selection. Frequently the devices carry the name of the physician who invented them. In very unstable fractures, a displacement osteotomy is occasionally performed.

Occasionally a physical therapy technician may come across a patient who has suffered a hip fracture but did not require an internal fixation. Such a patient has suffered an intertrochanteric fracture in which the distal and proximal fragments were impacted into each other and therefore afforded some stability of the fracture fragments. This condition is rare, however.

Physical Therapy after Hip Operations

For a good functional outcome of the various hip joint operations, the postoperative physical therapy and ambulation program is of utmost importance.

The physical therapy technician must stay exactly within the guidelines and instructions given to him by the physical therapist he is assigned to. It is the physical therapist who will interpret the guidelines given to him by the physician who is in charge of the patient. Any omission of a safety procedure may jeopardize the patient's welfare and can invite serious complications. For instance, if a patient falls because he was not sufficiently assisted or watched during his early walking trials, the internal fixation devices can become loosened, or the patient may break the other hip. In the case of a patient who has undergone an osteotomy, forceful twisting of the operated leg may impair the alignment of the bone fragments. Especially after hip surgery, caution is important. The patient now has all the potential to become ambulatory and independent of the physical assistance of family members. A fall or an awkward bodily maneuver could cause damage that would restrict the patient again to a wheelchair or bed. Should you have any doubt about the activities you have been assigned to perform with the patient, you must clarify the orders with your therapist. In an instance when it is absolutely necessary to leave your patient's side, you must bring him to a safe and comfortable lying or sitting position first. Under no circumstances leave the patient standing in parallel bars or on crutches with no one watching him. A patient also frequently has to be assisted when sitting down. He should not flop into the chair.

In this chapter you will find a general outline of the postoperative ambulation program for patients who have had an internal fixation or a prosthetic replacement of a hip joint. The postoperative ambulation plan has to be tailored individually to each patient. It will be outlined by the physician to the physical therapist. The therapist, in turn, will assign certain activities to the therapy technician. The exact interpretation of the physician's orders is the therapist's responsibility.

Postoperative Ambulation Plan in Hip Operations

Patients are usually permitted to sit up and dangle their legs on the fourth or fifth postoperative day and then to stand, using the walker, on the next day, without bearing any weight on the operated side. Strengthening exercises to the upper extremities, mainly arm extensors and shoulder depressors, should have been performed by the patient prior to ambulation with the walker. These exercises are mentioned in Chapter 8. Further increase in activity is regulated individually and varied according to the patient's general physical condition and other aspects of the recovery. The length of hospitalization after a hip operation usually is 3–4 weeks. At the time of discharge, the patients usually are walking with two crutches and bear partial weight on the leg that has been operated on.

Patients with total hip replacement are usually not allowed any activity which places stress on the operated hip, other than partial weight bearing, until the greater trochanter of the operated leg is judged by the orthopedic surgeon to be uniting satisfactorily. This usually occurs 6 weeks after the operation. During a total hip replacement it is often necessary to remove the trochanter from the femur together with the hip abductor muscles that insert in the trochanter. When the patient puts weight on the operated leg, a contraction of the hip abductor muscle is necessary to keep the pelvis horizontal while the other leg is in swing phase. The abductor muscles pull on the greater trochanter and could pull off the surgical fixation on the femur if full weight bearing is allowed too early. After the trochanter of the operated leg has united sufficiently with the femur, the patients are permitted to increase their activity and the amount of weight bearing. There are considerable variations, depending not only on the speed of recovery of the hip but also on the patient's general physical condition and age.

The physician may order strengthening exercises, that is, exercises against resistance, to improve hip muscle control. These muscles are frequently weakened because of disuse prior to the operation and bed rest and non-weight bearing after the operation. The time required to become free of pain, to regain muscle control, resume weight bearing and discard walking aids depends on many factors. In total hip replacement the recovery time is usually no longer than in any other type of hip replacement.

Changes of Gait after Hip Surgery

Most of the patients who have undergone some form of hip replacement will say the hip is much less painful. This is a subjective statement, however. There are other, more objective signs which show improvement; for example, the patients are able to put on and remove shoes and stockings and to bend down, to drive a car without discomfort and to perform the general activities of daily living much more easily. The range of hip motion, which usually was reduced in three planes, that is, flexion-extension, abduction-adduction and inward and outward rotation, is improved in most patients after reconstructive hip surgery.[4]

Fig. 7-11.—Varus deformity.

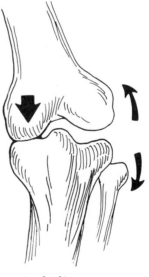

Left Knee

The hip abductor and sometimes also the hip adductor muscles have frequently been weakened for a long time prior to hip surgery. This is mostly weakness from disuse. Pain in the hip joint forbade motion and proper weight-bearing in stance phase, which would have caused a strong contracture of the abductor muscles. There may also be a slight change in the distance between the pelvis and greater trochanter after hip surgery. This alone can affect the contraction force of the hip muscles. Also, as mentioned in Chapter 5, there is a shift of the line of gravity toward the involved side just prior to the stance phase in patients with unilateral hip involvement. In some of the patients this shift disappears. However, in some patients it remains.[2]

There are other measurable changes that indicate that the patient has benefited from the surgery. Most patients are able to walk faster after surgery. They increase the walking speed by taking longer strides with greater rapidity. The patients who had an unequal stance period prior to surgery may decrease the difference between the stance phase in the good and in the bad hip. In some patients the stance periods become completely equal. (In unilateral hip pain, the stance phase on the painful side is shorter in order to eliminate as much as possible increased pain during the weight-bearing phase. This has already been

Fig. 7-12.—Tibial wedge osteotomy.

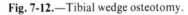

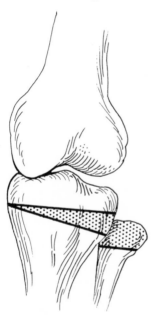
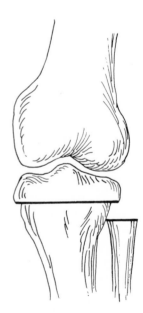

discussed in Chapter 5.) Another objective sign of the patient's improvement is the decrease in the use of walking aids, for instance, from two to one axillary crutches, or even to the use of a cane only. Some patients ambulate eventually without any walking aid.

In hip fractures it is difficult to make any pre- and postoperative comparative measurements of hip function. Most patients who have suffered a hip fracture that was stabilized with internal fixation are eventually able to walk with a cane and only a slight limp. Some can ambulate without any walking aid. Even at best, however, the measurements of hip muscle function on the operated side do not become normal. This is of little importance. The crucial point is that the patient can walk independently and can enjoy life.

Corrective Knee Operations

After the hips, the largest weight-bearing joints are the knees. Frequently osteoarthritis in these joints hampers the walking ability of the elderly. Persons who are overweight are more frequently afflicted

Fig. 7-13.—Valgus deformity.

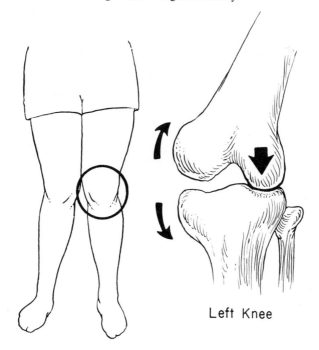

Left Knee

with knee disorders than are persons of normal weight. The knee becomes deformed and may develop some lateral instability. The deformity may progress to such a degree that it becomes a *varus* (Latin, bent inward) or *valgus* (Latin, bent outward) deformity.

In the varus deformity the convexity is toward the lateral side (Fig. 7-11). All the weight-bearing stresses are carried by the medial part of the tibial plateau and by the medial condyle. The steady stress and pain cause some swelling. The orthopedic surgeon may have to correct this deformity with a so-called *tibial wedge osteotomy*. A lateral wedge is cut from the tibia, and the bones are stapled together with an internal fixation device (Fig. 7-12).

Occasionally we find a valgus deformity or knock-knee (Fig. 7-13). This deformity is rare, however. In this instance, all the weight-bearing stresses are carried by the lateral joint surfaces. A *medial wedge osteotomy* may have to be performed to distribute weight-bearing stress

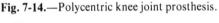

Fig. 7-14.—Polycentric knee joint prosthesis.

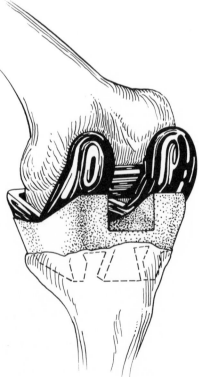

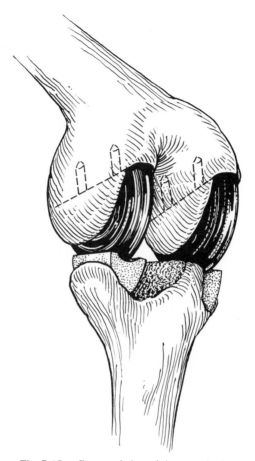

Fig. 7-15.—Geometric knee joint prosthesis.

equally to the medial and lateral joint surface. For valgus deformity of the knee a *femoral osteotomy* is sometimes performed. A wedge, with the apex pointing laterally, is removed from the femur just above the condyles. The proximal and distal fragments are fixed together with metal nail and plate.

Principally, the tibial and low femoral osteotomy are performed for the same purpose in knee joint disease as the previously described femoral osteotomy in hip joint disease. The goal is to change and redistribute the weight-bearing stresses on the joint surfaces.

In rheumatoid arthritis, the lining of the knee joint, the *synovial membrane,* may become so thickened that it restricts joint motion. Its chemical action begins to destroy the bearing surface of the joint, the articular cartilage. A *synovectomy* (*synovia* + Greek *ektome*, excision), in which the thickened synovium is removed, is done to free the joint and help prevent further joint cartilage destruction.

During the past decade, attempts have been made to insert a total knee replacement for advanced knee joint destruction. The indications for knee joint replacement and the benefits the patient derives from it are not so clear as those for total hip replacement. A physical therapy technician may, however, encounter a patient who has undergone a total knee joint replacement or a replacement of parts of the knee joint. At present the most frequently used artificial knees are the *polycentric* total knee (Fig. 7-14) and the *geometric* total knee (Fig. 7-15). In both types the convex femoral components are made of the metal Vitallium, and the concave tibial components are made of plastic.

Physical Therapy and Ambulation for Osteotomy and Synovectomy about the Knee

The patient starts usually with quadriceps contractions and flexion and extension exercises. About 1 week after surgery, ambulation with walking aids is started, without weight bearing on the operated leg. After 1–2 weeks, crutch walking with partial weight bearing on the operated side can be started. After 4–6 weeks, progressive resistive exercises to the quadriceps with straight leg raising can be initiated. Most patients who have undergone a tibial or lower femoral osteotomy or a synovectomy can walk eventually with the support of a regular cane or without any assistive device.

Bilateral Leg Impairment

In cases where the patient has an impairment in both extremities and is not allowed to bear full weight on only one extremity at any moment of the gait cycle, he has to be taught a two-point or four-point gait, as described in Chapter 8.

REFERENCES

1. Charnley, John: The bonding of prosthesis to bone by cement, J. Bone & Joint Surg. 46B:158, 1964.
2. Wilson, P. D., Jr., *et al:* Total hip replacement with fixation by acrylic cement, J. Bone & Joint Surg. 54A:207, 1972.
3. Patterson, F. P.: The McKee-Farrar total hip replacement, J. Bone & Joint Surg. 54A:257, 1972.
4. American Academy of Orthopaedic Surgeons: *Joint Motion: Method of Measuring and Recording* (Chicago: American Academy of Orthopaedic Surgeons, 1965).

CHAPTER **8**

AMBULATION AIDS

Ambulation (Latin *ambulare,* to move from place to place, to walk) is a functional activity for which some patients must be physically prepared. Patients who have an impairment of the lower extremities frequently need a mechanical device, as well as a certain physical strength, to enable them to ambulate. The type of mechanical walking aid depends on the patient's disability. Ambulation aids are prescribed by the physician after careful evaluation of the patient's general condition and the specific gait disability.

Under the guidance of a physical therapist, the physical therapy technician introduces the patient to the proper use of these mechanical aids. These devices enable the patient to help himself with his arms and hands in locomotion on level ground, stairs and inclines.

Some patients may have been so weakened by disease or prolonged bed rest that a preambulation therapy program may be required before ambulation training begins. Preambulation programs may consist of range-of-motion exercises and strengthening exercises to the upper extremities, mainly to the muscles that extend the elbow and those that depress the shoulder. These muscles are important for the use of walking aids. In the lower extremities, strengthening exercises to hip extensors and abductors and knee extensors are frequently necessary. In lower-extremity amputees, the abdominal muscles should also be strengthened.

Sometimes it is not advisable to bring a patient who has been lying down for a long time into the erect standing or sitting position immediately. A tilt table may have to be used. This preambulation aid consists of a tiltboard with a footrest and straps. It can be tilted from the horizontal to the vertical position manually or by an electromotor. The table is tilted to a higher degree daily, according to the patient's tolerance (Fig. 8-1). The supervising therapist has to check frequently for the patient's pulse rate. A sharp increase in the pulse rate indicates that the patient's tolerance for standing is still inadequate.

When a patient is ready for ambulation, he should first be dressed properly for the activity. His clothing should be securely fastened, and he must wear stockings and well-fitting shoes. *Do not ambulate barefoot patients.*

129

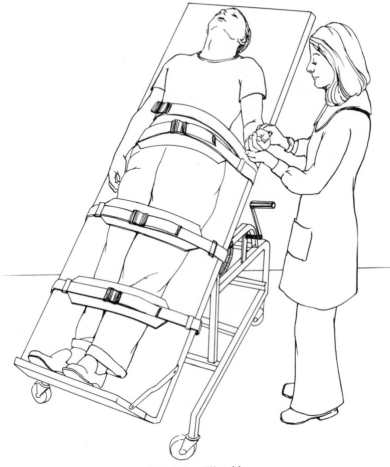

Fig. 8-1.—Tilt table.

Parallel Bars

The first step is usually ambulation in parallel bars (Fig. 8-2). These bars are very helpful in initial standing and walking. They are stable and give the patient the feeling of security. The patient actually propels himself forward more with the hands than with the legs. To induce him gradually to place more body weight on the lower extremities, he is encouraged to put the palm of the flat hand on the bars without gripping them at all. The height and width of the bars has to be adjusted to fit the individual patient. The height should be such that the elbows are bent

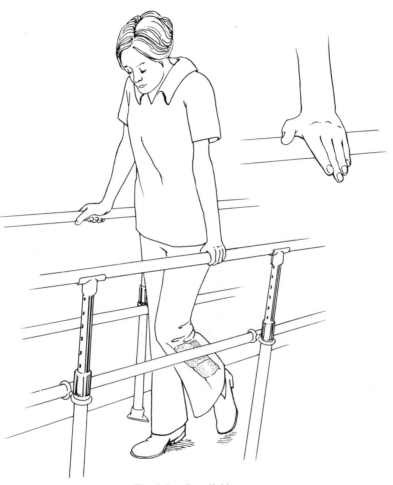

Fig. 8-2.—Parallel bars.

25–30 degrees when the patient is standing and holding onto the bars with his hands.

Walker

The next step is the use of a walker, which consists of a frame with four adjustable legs, usually made of aluminum (Fig. 8-3). Each of the legs must have a rubber tip to prevent sliding. The walker serves the same function as the parallel bars, but is not as stable. It can be used at

Fig. 8-3.—Walker.

home and on the ward and can be transported easily. The height has to be adjusted to the individual patient. The elbow should be flexed 25–30 degrees when the patient is standing with his hands on the walker.

In ambulation the walker is first lifted with both hands and then placed forward 25–30 cm. Then it is stepped into, first with the stronger and then with the weaker leg.

If the patient can bear weight only on one lower extremity, or has one leg amputated, he must place the walker forward and then lift up his body weight by pressing down on the walker while stepping into it with the weight-bearing extremity. The lifting of the body weight is done by the shoulder depressors and elbow extensors. As previously mentioned, these muscles have to be strengthened in some patients prior to ambulation.

The walker can be used only on level ground. It can be transported easily, but it is useless on stairs. A hinged walker is occasionally used for stair walking, but it does not offer as much stability as the standard walker.

The walker is helpful in the early stages of training for patients who will eventually go on to lesser aids like crutches or a cane. Frequently it is used, however, as a permanent walking aid for elderly people who are confined to their living quarters or have some balance difficulties.

Crutches

Once the patient is secure with the walker, he can be ambulated with so-called axillary crutches. Patients with good balance and strong upper extremities can be ambulated with crutches immediately, without the prior use of a walker.

The standard axillary crutches are wooden crutches, composed of two wooden uprights and an adjustable bottom secured to the uprights with two screws, an axillary crossbar joining the uprights at the upper end and a handgrip that can be adjusted (Fig. 8-4). The crutches also must be rubber-tipped at the bottom in order not to slip on the floor. In crutch walking, the patient shifts about 50% of the weight-bearing load from his legs to his arms and crutches.[1] The crutches have to be fitted to the individual patient. The distance from the patient's axilla to his heel plus 5 cm is the approximately correct length of the crutch. The handgrip is placed between the uprights so that the elbow is in 25–30-degree flexion. After the patient assumes the standing position with his crutches, the crutches may have to be readjusted.

In the standing position, the tips of the crutches are approximately 15–20 cm in front and 15–20 cm to the side of the toes. A tripod base is formed with the patient's feet and the crutches. To place the body center of gravity more toward the base of the tripod, the patient is asked to bring the hips forward. He also should look straight ahead in the direction he will walk, not down to the tip of the crutches and his feet. The axillary crossbar must *not* fit snug with the axilla; there should be approximately 3 cm, or the width of 2 fingers, between the crossbar and the axilla. The crossbar should lean toward the ribs for stabilization.

The patient must not bear weight on the axillary crossbar. If he bears weight or leans on the crossbar, there may be an impairment of the nerves or arteries that supply the arm and the hand. Should a patient complain of numbness in arms or hands, or feel his grip weakening, the physical therapy technician should notify the supervising therapist or the physician immediately. Numbness or weakness in arm or hand are early signs of crutch palsy. Patients with lower extremity involvement

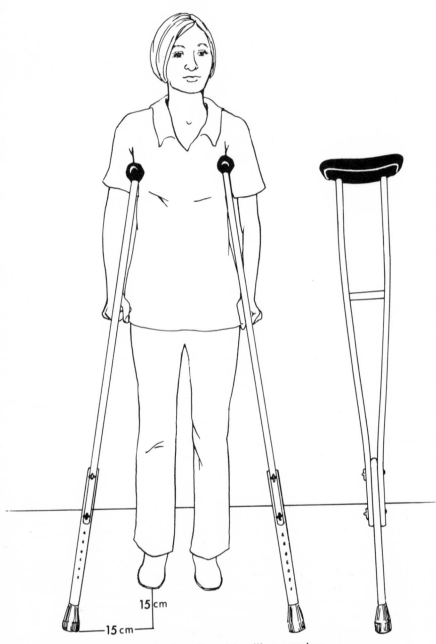

15 cm

—15 cm—

Fig. 8-4.—Standing with axillary crutches.

who suffer a crutch palsy may become severely disabled, since the use of mechanical walking aids requires well-functioning upper extremities. As mentioned previously, the handgrip should be adjusted so that there is approximately a 25–30-degree flexion at the elbow. This allows the body to be raised with the elbows extended when all the pressure and weight bearing is applied to the handgrip.

Different types of gait are used with crutches, depending on the patient's disability. If the patient has one normal lower limb which can tolerate full weight bearing, the crutches are moved forward with the affected limb. This is the so-called 3-point gait (Fig. 8-5). This mode of crutch walking is used, for instance, after hip or knee operations.

Another type of gait, the so-called four-point gait, is indicated for patients who are able to move their legs alternately but not to bear the full weight on either leg without the support of crutches (Fig. 8-6). Legs and crutches move in the sequence of left crutch-right foot-right crutch-left foot. When the patient is using the crutches in this manner, one can assume that he actually ambulates with four legs. In the four-point gait, only one leg or crutch is off the floor at a time, leaving three points for support, and this is therefore a very stable and safe gait.

Another form of crutch gait is the so-called two-point gait, which is a modification of the four-point gait. It is close to the natural rhythm of walking. The right crutch and left leg move together, and the left crutch and right leg move together (Fig. 8-7).

If the patient is paralyzed in both lower extremities and is unable to move the lower limbs alternately—for example, a paraparetic or paraplegic—the swing-to or swing-through gaits are used. When the patient has a flaccid paralysis of the lower extremities, the ankles and knees have to be stabilized with long leg braces to enable the patient to engage in these modes of crutch walking. For these gaits the patient has to have a good balance. Every precaution should be taken to ensure his safety while he is learning them. These gaits should first be taught in the parallel bars. They require very strong upper extremities and good coordination.

The following is a description of the so-called swing-to gait (Fig. 8-8). The patient assumes the previously described standing position and places his full body weight down on the handgrips of the crutches by extending his elbows. In standing position, the patient has to thrust the pelvis forward to place the center of gravity posterior to the hip joints. This forward thrust helps to prevent jackknifing in the hips when the hip extensor muscles are very weak. The patient's body is lifted and swings forward, and the feet are placed in line with the crutches. At that point both crutches are moved forward again. It is extremely important for the patient to move the crutches quickly, since he is not stable with feet and crutches in a straight line.

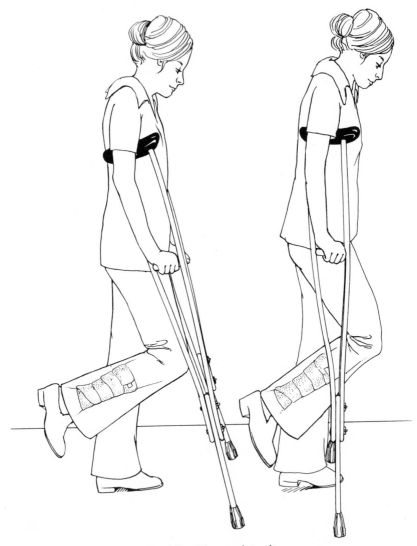

Fig. 8-5.—Three-point gait.

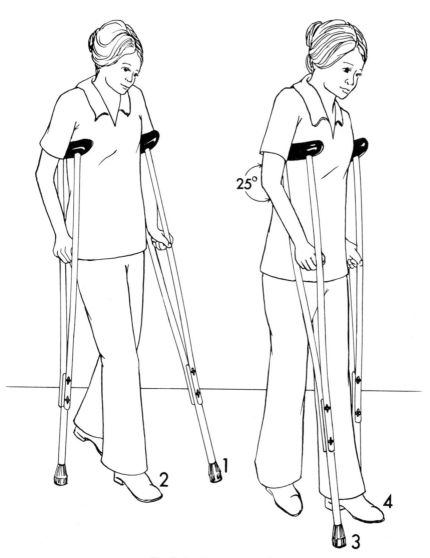

Fig. 8-6.—Four-point gait.

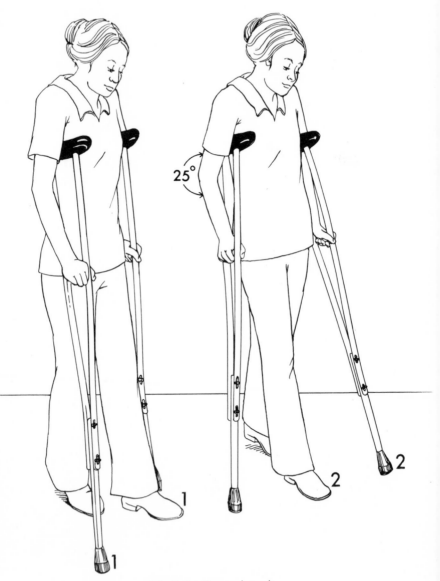

25°

1

2

2

1

Fig. 8-7.—Two-point gait.

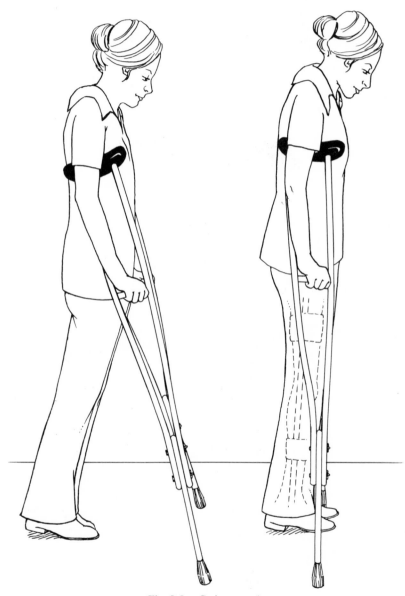

Fig. 8-8.—Swing-to gait.

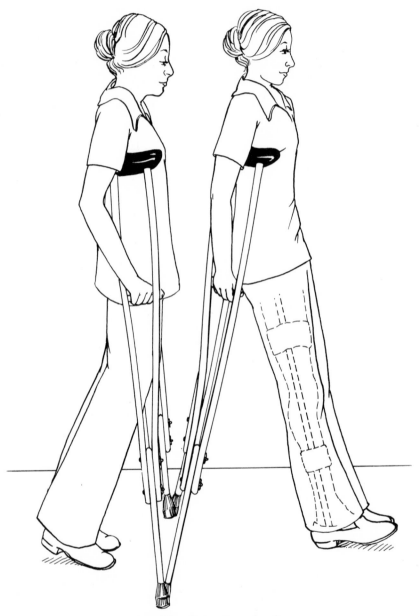

Fig. 8-9.—Swing-through gait.

The next, somewhat more difficult, gait is the so-called swing-through gait (Fig. 8-9). This gait is similar to the swing-to gait except that the feet are placed ahead of the crutches and then the crutches are brought in front of the feet again. This form of gait requires very strong shoulder and arm muscles and excellent balance. It is very fast, but can usually only be mastered by a young and strong patient.

Another problem in crutch walking is the use of a chair. Besides learning to walk with crutches, the patient also should be instructed in

Fig. 8-10.—Sitting down in chair.

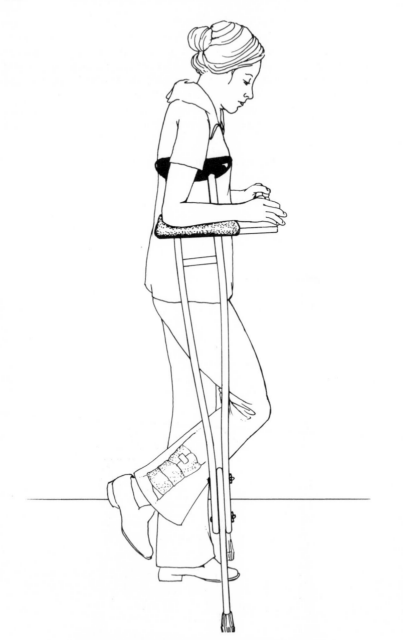

Fig. 8-11.—Axillary crutches with adaptive devices.

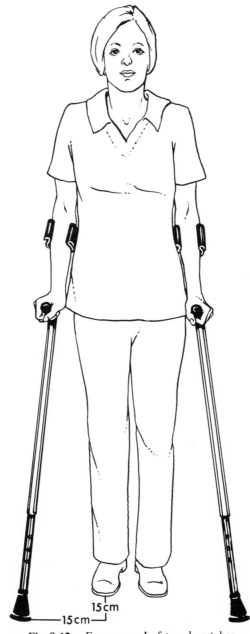

15cm

15cm

Fig. 8-12.—Forearm or Lofstrand crutches.

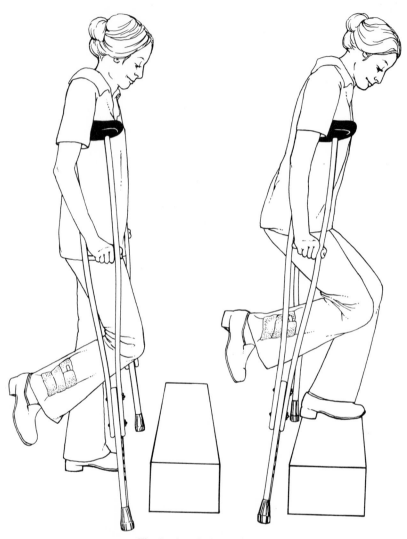

Fig. 8-13.—Going upstairs.

sitting down and standing up from chairs of varying height. These technics are best taught at the beginning of the crutch ambulation program so that the patient can practice them when he stops to rest during an ambulation session. The mode of getting into and out of a chair will depend on the type of chair and the patient's disability. The method safest for the patient is the preferable one. Some general guidelines have

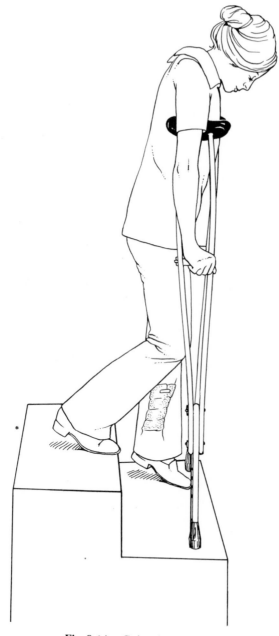

Fig. 8-14.—Going downstairs.

to be observed by patients when using a chair (Fig. 8-10):

1. The chair should be well supported and should not slide.
2. The crutches are removed from under the arm and held in one hand, freeing the other hand for support when he sits down.
3. With his free hand the patient should push directly down on the chair seat or armrest to support his weight.
4. Then he lowers himself into the chair by gradually flexing the elbow.
5. Standing up from a chair is accomplished in the reverse order of sitting down on the chair.

In the event the patient has some difficulty in maintaining a strong grip on the handgrip of the crutch, special adjustments can be made. The more common modifications are the shelf or platform crutch. Such a modification transfers the weight-bearing force from the hand to the ulnar side of the forearm. When the patient cannot extend the elbow for some reason, similar devices are used (Fig. 8-11).

Another frequently used type of crutches is the forearm or "Lofstrand" type, made of aluminum. From 40 to 50% of the body weight can be taken off the lower extremities when the crutches are used properly. These crutches give more support than a cane. Instead of one point of support, like the handgrip of a cane, the forearm crutch has two points, the handgrip and the forearm cuff (Fig. 8-12). Rubber tips prevent slipping on the floor. The forms of gait are the same as with axillary crutches.

In managing stairs, the stress is always on the leg that does the lifting of the body weight by extension in hip and knee. When walking upstairs, the good leg has to be placed on the next higher step first, while the ambulation aid supports the impaired leg on the step below. Walking aid and impaired leg have to be brought up together (Fig. 8-13). When walking downstairs, the impaired leg comes first together with the ambulation aid, while the good leg has to bear the body weight when flexing hip and knee (Fig. 8-14). Remember "Up with the good, and down with the bad." A strong grip on the stair rail with one hand and the ambulation aid in the other hand offers the most safety on stairs.

Canes

A cane is a convenient walking aid for relieving one extremity of some weight-bearing load, and it affords some stability. The cane is made of aluminum or wood, with a rounded handgrip to fit the hand better. A rubber suction tip prevents slipping. The rubber tip should be 2.5 cm in diameter. There are also canes with a straight horizontal handle available for people with arthritic deformities of the hands. The length of the cane should be adjusted so that the elbow is bent 25–30 degrees when standing with the cane (Fig. 8-15). In most physical therapy departments adjustable aluminum canes are available for training and measuring.

Frequently it is held that a patient who needs a cane only for the support of ambulation can also walk without it. This does not hold up in practice, however. Many elderly people with locomotion difficulties are afforded a safe gait with a cane. The cane should be used in the hand opposite the impaired leg. There are important kinesiologic and mechanical reasons for using the opposite hand. First, the leg and opposite arm move together in normal walking. Second, a wider base is provided to increase stability. Third, the shift of the center of gravity from 1 side to the other is eliminated. The center of gravity must always be between the mechanical ambulation aid and the leg it is supporting. For instance, in a right-leg disability the cane should be held in the left hand. The center of gravity is between the right leg and the cane in the left hand. If the cane were used wrongly in the right hand to support the right leg, the center of gravity would be between the right leg and the cane and would therefore move further away from the midline of the body, and more weight would be put on the impaired leg.

Besides the shift of the body weight to the unimpaired leg, there is another mechanical advantage in using a cane or crutch in the opposite hand as a walking aid. During unsupported walking another force is acting on the hips besides the weight. The hip abductor muscles contract and press on the hip to keep the pelvis from tilting when the opposite leg is in the swing phase and does not support the pelvis. An ambulation aid on the opposite side therefore takes more stress off the hip than just part of the body weight (Fig. 8-16).[2]

A cane is also very useful for persons who have spells of dizziness and momentary loss of balance. This does occur in elderly persons. The cane gives these persons some means to control the momentary unsteadiness in case there is no wall or furniture to lean against.

When we speak of a cane, we usually understand a unilateral walking aid. Therefore, an axillary or forearm crutch can be used like a cane. When these are used properly, 20–30 lb of stress are placed on a cane, and about 40 lb of stress on the forearm crutch.[3]

To assure more stability in elderly people, a three- or four-legged cane can be used. This is very useful on level ground, but it allows only a slow gait. When the patient tries to walk faster, a rocking action from the two rear legs to the front legs or leg develops. This rocking action defeats the goal of increased stability. A 3- or 4-legged cane is very

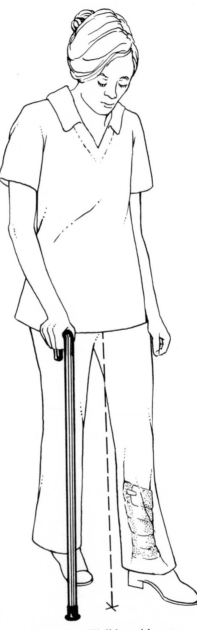

Fig. 8-15.—Walking with a cane.

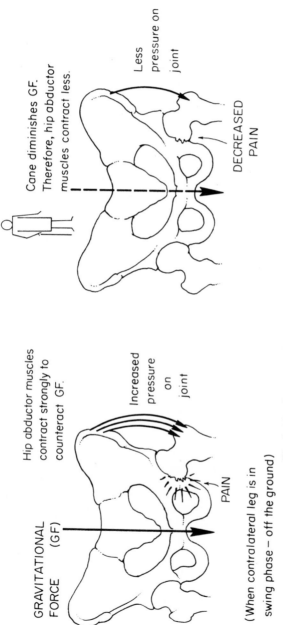

Fig. 8-16.—Leverage forces with unilateral walking aid.

Fig. 8-17.—Three- and four-legged canes.

useful for elderly people, however, since they have a slow gait anyway and use the cane mostly for increased stability. People who suffer from hemiparesis after a stroke often benefit from this form of device. This type of cane can only be used on stairs with very wide and very low steps (Fig. 8-17).

Another walking aid that is used as a cane is the so-called reversed or hemiwalker. The patient holds the walker like a cane, on the opposite side with one hand. Increased stability is gained, but the patient can only ambulate slowly. The walker has four points of contact with the floor, but again, a faster gait would result in a rocking motion that would eliminate the stabilizing factor (Fig. 8-18). It can be used only on level ground or on stairs with very wide and low steps.

The height of all these walking aids should be adjusted to such a level that the elbow is flexed at 25–30 degrees when the patient is standing with his walking aid.

Always remember to check any ambulation aid before giving it to a patient. Assure yourself that the rubber tips which prevent slipping on the floor are correctly applied and that none of the fastening screws are loose.

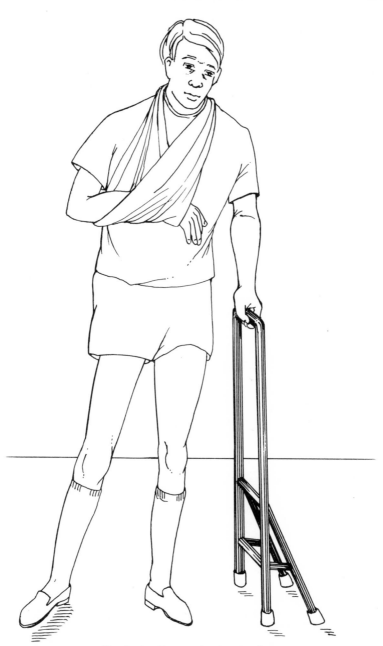

Fig. 8-18.—Reversed or hemiwalker.

REFERENCES

1. Jebsen, R. H.: Use and abuse of ambulation aids, JAMA 199:68, 1967.
2. Blount, W. P.: Don't throw away the cane, J. Bone & Joint Surg. 38A:695, 1956.
3. Robinson, H. S.: Cane measurement and recording of stress, Arch. Phys. Med. 50:457, 1969.

CHAPTER 9

AMBULATION PROBLEMS
IN AMPUTEES

With the increase in longevity, more of the elderly suffer from an insufficiency of blood supply to the lower extremities as the blood vessels become rigid and clogged. Progress in peripheral vascular surgery enables the surgeon to correct this problem sometimes by the insertion of a piece of vein or synthetic material to bypass a clogged artery. In some patients, however, there is a diffuse narrowing of the blood vessel lumen, and the distal parts of the leg do not receive enough blood. The leg becomes cold, discolored, very painful and often *necrotic* (from Greek *necrosis,* deadness). Eventually the patient has to be relieved of his pain by an *amputation* (Latin *amputare,* to cut off or to prune). Insufficient blood supply is the most frequent cause, but other pathology, such as a tumor or injury, may require the amputation of a leg. Some patients have an obstruction of the blood supply to both lower limbs, and may need to have both legs amputated.

This chapter deals only with amputations of the lower limbs. Amputation of an arm or hand is much less frequent. It is hardly ever done because of vascular insufficiency, but rather as a sequel of industrial and war injuries or of congenital defects. Rehabilitation and prosthetic appliances for the arms will not be discussed here. Training with upper extremity prostheses requires the skill of very experienced occupational and physical therapists.

The postoperative care and gait training of leg amputees also needs the skill and knowledge of an experienced physical therapist. Certain specific activities in gait training can be assigned, however, by the physical therapist to be performed by the physical therapy technician.

Levels of Amputations

Depending on the severity and type of blood flow obstruction, an amputation may be performed above the knee, below the knee or at the ankle. The surgeon tries to save as much of the limb as possible. Some blood flow has to be present at the level of the amputation site to secure proper healing.

Corresponding to the level of the amputation site, we speak of hip disarticulation, above-knee and below-knee amputations and amputations about the ankle. Above-knee and below-knee amputations are the most frequent operations.

Hip Disarticulation

A hip disarticulation is mostly performed when the entire lower extremity has to be amputated because of a malignant tumor. The power to move the prosthesis has to come, therefore, from the movement between pelvis and lumbar spine. Forward tilting of the pelvis in swing phase moves the prosthesis forward. During the stance phase the body weight has to be borne by the pelvic area when the patient wears the prosthesis.

Above-Knee Amputations

According to the length of the stump, the above-knee amputations are divided into short above-knee stump, midthigh stump, long above-knee stump and end-bearing above-knee stump.

SHORT ABOVE-KNEE STUMP.—When the amputation level is between an area 5 cm below the perineum and the lower border of the upper third of the thigh, we speak of a short above-knee stump. The perineum is the area between the symphysis pubis and the lower end of the sacrum. The main force for moving the prosthesis comes, again, from the motion between the pelvis and the lumbar spine. Most of the weight is transferred by the ischial tuberosity onto the prosthesis.

MIDTHIGH STUMP.—The midthigh amputation, within the middle third of the thigh, is 1 of the more frequently performed ones. The main force for moving the prosthesis comes from the motion between the femoral head and the acetabulum. The remaining part of the thighbone brings the prosthetic socket forward in swing phase by contracting the hip flexor muscles, and stabilizes the hip in stance phase by contraction of the hip extensor muscles. Again, the weight is transferred through the ischial tuberosity onto the prosthesis.

LONG ABOVE-KNEE STUMP.—The stump ends below the middle of the thigh. The mechanics of moving the prosthetic socket are nearly the same as with midthigh amputation. There is one advantage, however. The longer thighbone gives better leverage for the action of the hip extensor and hip flexor muscles. The weight is borne by the ischial tuberosity.

END-BEARING ABOVE-KNEE STUMP.—In the previously listed amputations, the major portion of the body weight is transferred from the ischial tuberosity to the prosthetic socket. No weight is borne by the end surface of the stump.

Amputations at the knee joint or through the femoral condyles furnish a stump that can tolerate some weight bearing at the end. These amputations are often called Gritti-Stokes, after the physicians who first described them. Compared with midthigh amputations, the Gritti-Stokes amputations are much more seldom performed.

Below-Knee Amputations

These amputations are divided into short below-knee stump and standard below-knee stump.

SHORT BELOW-KNEE STUMP.—In this stump the tibia is not longer than 5 cm. The main weight is carried between the patella ligament, the flares of the tibial condyles and the anteromedial wall of the tibia. The power to move the prosthesis is supplied by the action of the quadriceps and hamstring muscles.

STANDARD BELOW-KNEE STUMP.—The amputation level for the tibia is between an area 5 cm below the top of the tibia and the area where the gastrocnemius muscle unites with the Achilles tendon. The prosthesis is moved by the flexion and extension action of the hamstrings and quadriceps. The weight is transferred onto the prosthesis by the patella tendon.

Amputations about the Ankle

The most frequent one is Syme's amputation (James Syme, a Scottish surgeon). The foot and ankle are removed, but the shank, or tibia, is not shortened. There is another advantage. Syme's amputation is designed in such a manner that the patient keeps his own heel pad, which is very resistant to pressure, as a weight-bearing surface (Fig. 9-1). In addition, a person with a Syme's amputation can walk in the house without an artificial limb. His own heel pad bears all the weight.

Preprosthetic Care

In earlier days it was customary to confine a patient to bed till the wound of the amputation site had healed. Extreme care had to be taken to avoid flexion contractures of the stump at the hip. After the sutures were removed, the stump had to be wrapped daily with an Ace bandage. The patient was then ambulated with axillary crutches or a walker, as indicated. Only after 4–6 weeks could the patient be measured for a permanent artificial limb. He then had to undergo gait training for 3–4 weeks. Nowadays, amputees are ambulated much earlier.

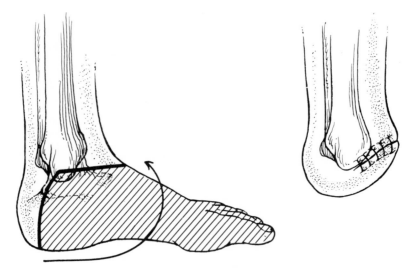

Fig. 9-1.—Syme's amputation stump.

It is a widely accepted practice to apply to the stump a plaster of paris cast dressing on the operating table, as soon as the last suture is made. Frequently an attachment that allows connection with a temporary artificial limb is included in the plaster cast (Fig. 9-2). This procedure can be used for both above-knee and below-knee amputations. Some patients are ambulated a few days after surgery and already place some weight on the temporary artificial limb. The rigid plaster cast is also used in ankle disarticulation (Syme's amputation). This form of management avoids the hazards of long bed rest, and edema in the stump is prevented to a large extent.

In patients with very severe vascular impairment or with potentially infected amputation sites, a rigid plaster dressing cannot be used. In these instances a *pylon* (temporary limb) with an ischial weight-bearing socket is used to ambulate the patient as soon as the sutures are removed, that is, approximately 10–12 days after surgery. Such a temporary prosthesis consists of a quadrilateral socket, made out of plastics or a plaster cast, and attached to an adjustable shank and prosthetic foot (Fig. 9-3). The posterior crest of the quadrilateral socket has a notch in which the ischial tuberosity rests and which also transfers the body weight onto the pylon. The skin around the ischial tuberosity is resistant to pressure and does not become painful and break down. This form of postoperative management reduces the waiting period between surgery and fitting for a permanent artificial limb. Instead of 4–6 weeks, it is 14–20 days. In addition, the period of gait training with

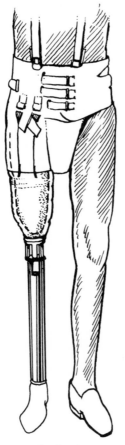

Fig. 9-2.—Temporary prosthesis: plaster cast with attachment.

the permanent artificial limb is substantially shortened, because the patient has already acquired some skill in artificial-limb walking from using the temporary appliance.

Prosthetics for the Lower-Limb Amputee

The future walking ability of the patient is assessed at an early stage.

There are many different types of artificial limbs, and each amputee is fitted with the one considered most suitable for him. The following factors have some bearing on the prosthetic prescription:

AGE AND GENERAL HEALTH OF THE PATIENT.—The patient's balance

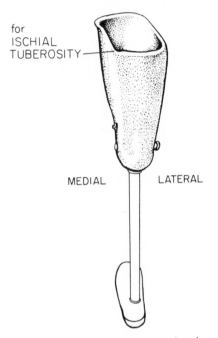

for
ISCHIAL
TUBEROSITY

MEDIAL   LATERAL

Fig. 9-3.—Pylon with quadrilateral socket.

and walking ability are the basis for giving an elderly patient a free or a locked knee, or deciding whether a prosthesis is warranted at all. Patients who are not self-directing or are generally too weak to walk should not be given an artificial limb. The patient's eyesight also has to be adequate to enable him to put on and take off the artificial limb.

Whenever there are some potentials for ambulation and the patient desires an artificial limb, a limb is usually prescribed for the patient. In patients with heart disease, ambulation with an artificial limb places less stress on the heart than hopping on one leg with a walker or crutch walking without a prosthesis. For the elderly, safety and comfort, not walking speed and gait appearance, are the prime consideration.

LENGTH OF THE STUMP.—The length of the stump influences the prosthetic prescription mainly as it relates to the form of the socket. For instance, a patient with an extremely short above-knee stump may not be able to drive the prosthesis. He may need a hip disarticulation prosthesis, or he may not be able to be fitted at all.

STUMP SKIN AND STUMP CIRCULATION.—The patient's stump skin and circulation influence the decision whether or not a suction socket should be considered. When the skin and circulation are poor, or an above-knee stump has scars from previous vascular surgery, a total-contact suction socket cannot be used. The patient has to wear stump socks and an auxiliary support around the waist.

Prosthesis for Amputations about the Hip

For amputations about the hip, even when the neck of the femur and the greater trochanter have been left intact, a hip disarticulation prosthesis or so-called Canadian hip prosthesis is used. While the movement at the hip joint does not serve any useful function, the firm piece of bone does help to make a more stable fitting of the prosthetic socket onto the pelvis.

A patient who has had to undergo a hemipelvectomy is fitted with essentially the same prosthesis. There is a different design of the socket, however. Because of the absence of a rigid bony pelvic structure, the socket has to be designed so that the support can be carried through the pliable abdominal wall. In some cases the socket has to be so designed that even a part of the bony structure of the thorax is used to increase the stability.

In a Canadian hip prosthesis, the artificial hip is mounted on the front surface of the socket to facilitate sitting for the prosthesis wearer (Fig. 9-4). To stabilize the hip, it is connected with an elastic strap that is fixed at the rear side of the socket and inserts in front of the knee in the shank. The location of the hip in relation to the socket and the attachment of the elastic strap in relation to hip and knee explain the stability of the prosthetic joint when in stance phase. In order to have stability when the prosthesis is in stance phase, the load or plumb line from the hip joint to the ankle joint has to pass in front of the knee joint. Therefore, the knee joint has to be set posterior to the prosthetic hip and ankle joint. If the load line were to pass posterior to the knee joint, the prosthetic knee would buckle in stance phase. With this form of prosthesis, most of the time a constant-friction knee is used, which means that the friction in the knee does not change with swing or stance phase.[1]

For a prosthetic foot, a single-axis conventional or a SACH foot is used.

The single-axis conventional foot consists of a solid wooden block. The ankle joint and toe sections are separately attached (Fig. 9-5). The ankle axis consists of a horizontal shaft that rotates on bushings. It gives plantar flexion and dorsiflexion only. There are also 2 rubber bumpers to restrain the motion in the ankle axis and prevent the prosthetic foot from turning loosely up and down.

Another frequently prescribed prosthetic foot is the SACH foot

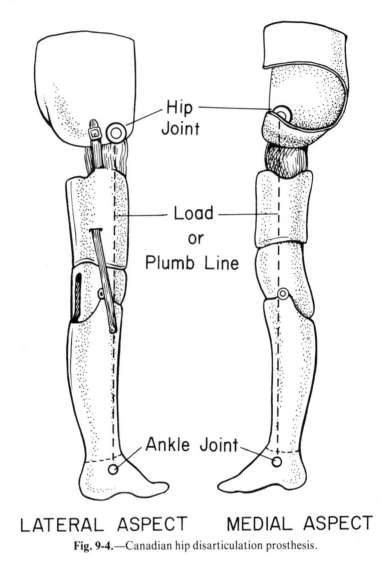

LATERAL ASPECT   MEDIAL ASPECT

Fig. 9-4.—Canadian hip disarticulation prosthesis.

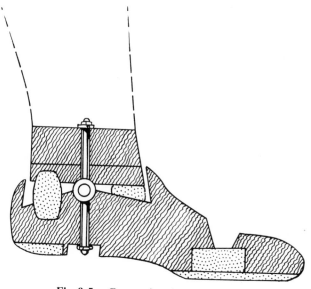

Fig. 9-5.—Conventional prosthetic foot.

Fig. 9-6.—SACH foot.

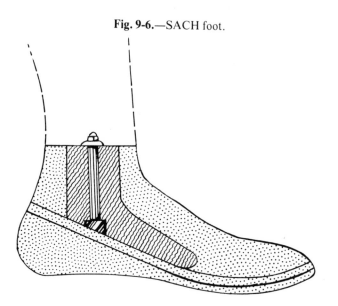

(SACH = *S*olid *A*nkle *C*ushion *H*eel). Rubber is molded over a wooden or metal heel. By compression of the rubber, the foot functions as if there were active eversion and inversion as well as plantar flexion and dorsiflexion (Fig. 9-6). There is no ankle joint. The prosthetic shaft is fixed to the prosthetic foot.

Prosthesis for Above-Knee Amputation

The quadrilateral socket is the most widely used form of socket at the present time (Fig. 9-7). The posterior surface is flat to facilitate sitting. The medial corner is carved out to make room for the bellies of the adductor muscles when these are contracting. The crest of the posterior wall has also a notch in which the ischial tuberosity will sit when the leg is in midstance phase. The inner side of the anterior wall is concave to accommodate the quadriceps muscle. The crest of the anterior wall is higher to furnish some counterpressure.

The above-knee prosthesis is often suspended by suction. The stump is fitted so tightly that a negative pressure develops when the prosthesis is in swing phase and off the ground (Fig. 9-8). At the distal end of the socket there is a valve which is open to let the air escape when the socket is donned. As soon as the socket is adjusted, the valve is closed by hand. To prevent wrinkles of the stump skin, the patient pulls a thin sock over the stump. After the socket is donned, he pulls the sock out through the valve opening at the distal end of the prosthesis to flatten the skin.

Fig. 9-7.—Quadrilateral socket.

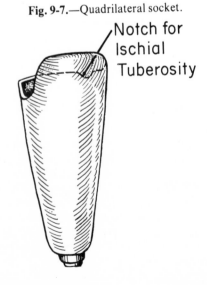

Notch for
Ischial
Tuberosity

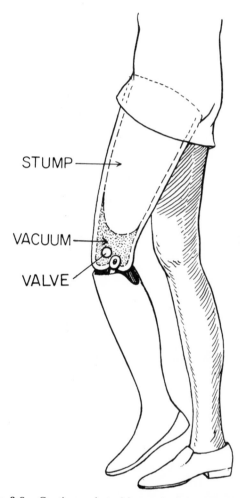

Fig. 9-8.—Suction socket with prosthetic knee and foot.

In a total contact socket, no stump sock is usually worn. There are three distinct advantages to a total contact suction socket:

1. There is no necessity for additional supportive devices such as a pelvic belt (Fig. 9-9) or a Silesian band (Fig. 9-10), which sometimes feel uncomfortable around the waist.

2. There is also a decrease in piston action. The piston action is the movement between stump and socket. In stance phase the stump sinks in deeper, and in swing phase the weight of the prosthesis makes it slide off the stump slightly.

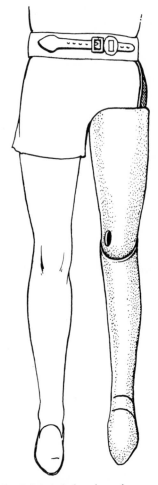

Fig. 9-9.—Pelvic belt for above-knee prosthesis.

3. In addition, due to the negative pressure, suction sockets feel more comfortable, and they do feel much lighter.

In older people, and many of the above-knee amputees are elderly, some of the previously mentioned additional support is necessary. Sometimes the skin in older patients is not resilient enough to have a total contact suction socket. An air flow valve can still be used, since some negative pressure will develop in swing phase when the valve is closed, and this makes the prosthesis feel much lighter. Many elderly people complain about the heavy weight of their prosthetic devices. A "partial suction" socket does eliminate this feeling.

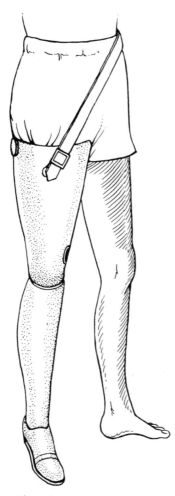

Fig. 9-10.—Above-knee prosthesis with Silesian band.

Weakened older patients frequently have difficulties in donning a suction socket. The pulling of the stump sock through the valve opening is quite strenuous, and many elderly people cannot perform it. They also may experience discomfort when bending forward to remove a tight-fitting suction socket. Often these patients have a heart disease and should not perform this rather strenuous maneuver.

An important part of the above-knee amputation prosthesis is the design of the artificial knee joint. Various types are available, ranging from the single-axis friction knee to the hydraulic knee. One feature is common to all types of prosthetic knees. The axis has to be posterior to the axis of the hip and the ankle. This form of alignment does afford stability of the knee in stance phase. The load line has to pass in front of the knee.

In some patients who have impaired balance, more stability is achieved when the prosthetic knee is locked in extension. The lock is usually a semiautomatic one. When the patient stands up, the knee locks automatically in extension. When he sits down, the patient unlocks it with his hand.

Prosthesis for Below-Knee Amputation

The majority of patients who have undergone a below-knee amputation have the level of the amputation at the upper border of the middle third of the tibia. The knee flexors and knee extensors have their insertion above this level and can maintain a well-functioning knee.

Since 1958, most patients with a below-knee amputation can be fitted with a PTB (*Patella Tendon Bearing*) prosthesis, which was developed by the Biomechanics Laboratory of the University of California. The part of the tendon below the *patella* (Latin, diminutive of *patera,* a shallow dish), like the ischial tuberosity, is very resistant and can take pressure without becoming painful. In the PTB prosthesis, no lacers or hinges are used. The sides of the socket are higher to give more lateral stability (Fig. 9-11). The patient actually kneels with 7 to 10 degrees of flexion in the prosthesis. The upper part of the gastrocnemius (calf muscle) does give some counterpressure.

The prosthesis is generally suspended by a simple cuff or strap around the thigh just above the kneecap. Occasionally it is suspended by a strap fixed on a waist belt. There are several modifications available. In some of these there is a window for the patella, and medial and lateral side bars are molded over the femoral condyles.

The foot most often used for the PTB prosthesis is the SACH foot or the conventional single-axis foot. Both of these prosthetic parts were described earlier in this chapter.

Prosthesis for Ankle Disarticulation
(Syme's Amputation)

For Syme's amputation, the Syme's prosthesis is used. It consists of a well-fitting plastic socket that is attached to a SACH foot. The socket reaches to just below the knee (Fig. 9-12).

The stump in a Syme's amputation is frequently bulbous, and therefore a window is made in the socket to facilitate the entry of the bulbous stump.

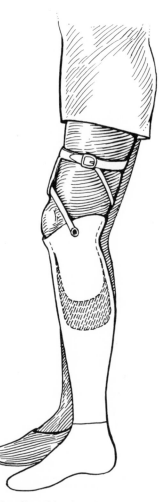

Fig. 9-11.—Patella tendon bearing (PTM) prosthesis.

Amputee Gait Training

The following is an outline of the walking training of an above-knee amputee. These comments about gait training serve as general guidelines only. The physical therapy technician will be assigned a specific task from day to day.

The pylon or prosthesis is applied when the patient is standing, leaning against the bed or other heavy and stable furniture. In below-

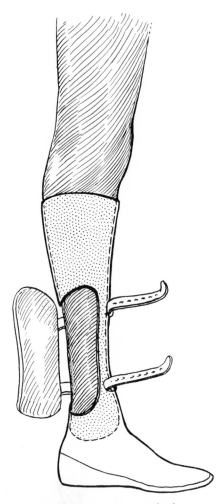

Fig. 9-12.—Syme's prosthesis.

knee amputees the prosthesis can also be applied in a sitting position. Talcum powder has to be applied prior to putting on the socks and the socket.

The patient begins training standing between parallel bars with his feet 20–25 cm apart in front of a mirror. He supports himself by holding the bars with his hands. Then the weight should be transferred from the sound leg to the artificial limb, and the reverse. This is practiced until full weight is taken on the artificial limb. The same maneuver should be repeated with the artificial limb first in front and then behind the sound leg in a step position. When this has been accomplished, walking in the parallel bars may begin. Care must be taken that the patient takes even steps. There is a tendency to take a long step with the artificial limb and a short one with the normal leg. When swinging the pylon forward to take a step, the patient uses the lateral flexors of the trunk, the so-called "hip hikers," to tilt the pelvis so that the pylon can clear the ground. The same applies when the patient is taught to walk with a locked prosthetic knee. By no means should he be allowed to swing the artificial limb or pylon out in circumduction, or raise himself onto the ball of the normal foot, the so-called "vaulting."

The length of time for which the artificial limb is worn should increase daily, starting with two periods of 1–2 hours in duration, and increasing until the limb is worn for the whole day. This is to allow the skin to become accustomed and hardened to the pressure of the socket. In case you notice redness in some area of the stump, notify your supervising therapist immediately. Many amputees have the habit of rubbing the stump immediately after the artificial limb is taken off. This may make the reddened pressure spots less distinct. Therefore, inspect the stump before the patient rubs it. If pressure areas do occur and the stump breaks down, the artificial limb should be left off until the skin is healed.

Once the patient is in command of walking in the parallel bars, he progresses to a four-point gait with two crutches (see Chapter 8). Afterwards he learns to walk with one crutch, and he should soon be able to manage with only a cane. Most elderly patients will always need some form of support. When walking without crutches, using a cane only, the arm should swing freely. Walking should also be practiced in front of the mirror so the patient can correct his own mistakes and gait deviations.

Further problems may be caused by a poorly fitting socket due to alterations in the stump since the first fitting. As the artificial limb is used more and more, further stump shrinkage usually occurs, and the prosthesis causes pressure on the proximal part of the adductor tendon in the groin. This can be relieved by using another stump sock. The shrinkage of the stump, which is caused by the pressure of the prosthesis, can be compensated for with a maximum of three woolen stump socks. In case this does not suffice, the lumen of the prosthetic socket has to be made smaller. In addition, stump swelling may prevent the body weight's being carried on the ischial tuberosity because the stump does not slide deep enough into the socket. This can be relieved only by leaving the artificial limb off until the swelling has gone. The disappearance of swelling can be hastened by firm bandaging of the stump when the limb is not worn.

When the patient trains for ambulation with a free-swinging prosthetic knee, he transfers his weight over to the normal leg and swings the prosthesis forward with the knee flexed to take a short step. The heel has to come in contact with the ground first to lock the knee. At this moment the patient has to extend the stump to stabilize the knee. Now his weight is over the prosthesis. The weight is next transferred back to the normal leg and the prosthesis brought back level with the good leg. This is practiced until the patient masters the knee action.

The next exercise is a progression of the previous one. Once the patient's weight is over the prosthesis, he swings his normal leg forward to take a step and gradually transfers his weight over to the normal leg. He then flexes his stump again, swings the prosthesis through with the knee flexed, brings the heel down to lock the knee and presses his stump back to stabilize the knee. The patient then starts to walk along between the parallel bars. After he ambulates well between the bars, he can proceed to crutches and cane.

One common fault when learning knee action is hip hiking in patients who were previously taught pylon walking. Another fault is exaggerating the swing-through and hitting the heel too hard on the floor to gain knee extension instead of using the extensor muscles of the stump.

The usual prosthesis of an elderly patient has a semiautomatic knee-lock mechanism. This is to aim at safety rather than a sightly gait. The patient will walk with a stiff knee, flexing the knee joint only for sitting down. Walking with a locked knee is like pylon walking. On standing up and with hip extension, a spring will cause the knee joint to straighten with an audible click, assuring that the patient's knee is fixed.

For single and bilateral below-knee amputations, gait training is much easier. Treatment consists of maintaining a normal walking gait.

With a Syme's amputation, the same is the case.

The below-knee amputee who is fitted with a PTB (Patella Tendon Bearing) prosthesis walks with the knee in 7 to 10 degrees of flexion.

After the patient can ambulate on level ground, he should be instructed in the following maneuvers:

WALKING SIDEWAYS.—The patient moves the crutch sideways and abducts the artificial limb, places it on the ground about 30 cm away and follows it with the normal leg. Then the process is reversed, beginning with the normal leg and following with the artificial limb.

MOVING BACKWARD.—The patient hikes the hip up, hyperextends the stump, brings the prosthesis backward and places it on the floor. In below-knee amputation, the knee is flexed to bring the prosthesis backward. The patient then moves the crutch backwards opposite the artificial limb and follows it with the normal leg and the other crutch.

TURNING A CORNER.—The patient is taught to take small steps with each foot, the good one and the prosthetic foot, and not just to pivot around the artificial limb. He must not turn on the spot.

WALKING UP AND DOWN AN INCLINE.—When going up, a long stride is taken with the normal leg and a short one with the artificial limb. The process is reversed in walking down an incline.

GOING UPSTAIRS AND DOWNSTAIRS.—Going upstairs, the normal foot takes the leading step. Coming down, the prosthesis leads (see Chapter 8).

SITTING AND RISING FROM A CHAIR.—To rise, the patient has to slide forward to the edge of the chair and then raise himself on the normal limb. To sit, the patient lowers himself on the chair with his weight on the normal leg. He can use the support of the armrest or back of the chair, if he needs it.

LOWERING ON AND RISING FROM THE FLOOR.—To lower himself to the floor, the patient hyperextends the stump and bends the normal knee, places the hands on the ground in line with the shoulders, rolls the trunk over to the sound side and then sits. To rise from the floor, he flexes the good knee, rotates the trunk toward the normal leg with the hands on the floor as before, puts his weight on the normal leg and straightens up.

PRACTICE IN FALLING.—The patient is encouraged to practice falling onto a mattress to help him lose some of his fear of falling and hurting himself. An amputee with an artificial limb is taught to fall on his hands, flexing the good knee. He then turns toward the side of the good knee to come into a sitting position. To get up, the patient should roll over to his hands and get up by straightening the good knee and hip.

When the patient is proficient in walking with the artificial limb and independent in daily activities, formal instruction should stop and the patient should be left on his own.

A regular checkup, about once a month, to stop any bad habits developing, is recommended. It is easier to prevent a bad habit than to break one.

The various technics of care for amputees and the prosthetic appliances have been improved strikingly within the last 25 years. The availability of new synthetic materials has enabled the prosthesis makers to produce lighter and better-functioning devices.

For the reader who wants to gain deeper insight into these problems, excellent instructive texts are available.[1-4]

REFERENCES

1. Humm, W.: *Rehabilitation of the Lower Limb Amputee* (2d ed.; Baltimore: Williams & Company, 1969).
2. Committee on Prosthetic-Orthotic Education, Division of Medical Sciences, National Research Council: *The Geriatric Amputee: Principles of Management* (Washington, D.C.: National Academy of Sciences, 1971).
3. Prosthetic and Sensory Aids Service, Department of Medicine and Surgery, Veterans Administration: *The Management of Lower Extremity Amputations* (Washington, D.C.: Superintendent of Documents, 1969).
4. Levy, S. W., and Barnes, G. H.: *Hygienic Problems of the Amputee* (Washington, D.C.: The American Orthotics and Prosthetics Association, 1961).

INDEX

V

Valgus deformity: knee, 125
Valves
  mitral, 40
  tricuspid, 40
Varus deformity: knee, 123
Veins, 38
Vena cava, 38
Ventricle, 39
Vertebra, 9
Vertebral column: anatomy, 9–11
Vessels, 40
Vocal cords, 42

W

Walker, 131–133
  hemiwalker, 151
  reversed, 151
Walking
  (*See also* Ambulation, Gait)
  cane (*see* Canes)

crutch (*see* Crutches)
incline, and amputees, 171
muscles and, 36–37
sideways, amputee, 170
Weight shift: in painful-hip gait, 77
Wheelchair transfers
  to bathtub, 103–106
  from bed
    assisted, standing, 91–93
    unassisted, sitting, 106–107, 109
    unassisted, standing, 89–91
  to car, 102–103
  to parallel bars, assisted, 93–94
  position of wheelchair relative to bed, 87
  to toilet, 98–102
  to treatment table, assisted, 94–95
Whirlpool, 62, 63
Wrist, 14
  motions, 21, 22